# Joy at the End of the Tether

# Joy
# at the End
# of the
# Tether

Douglas Wilson

Canon Press

MOSCOW, IDAHO

Douglas Wilson, *Joy at the End of the Tether: The Inscrutable Wisdom of Ecclesiastes*

© 1999 by Douglas Wilson
Published by Canon Press, P.O. Box 8741, Moscow, ID 83843
800-488-2034 / www.canonpress.org

05 04 03 02 01 99    9 8 7 6 5 4 3 2 1

Cover design by Paige Atwood Design, Moscow, ID

Printed in the United States of America.

ISBN: 1-885767-50-1

This book is dedicated, with a great deal of warm affection, to every fool in Christendom.

# Contents

# De Profundis

*Out of the depths have I cried unto thee, O LORD.*
                              Psalm 130:1

Our word *profound* comes from the Latin *profundus*, which means deep. Most cheerfulness in the world is quite the opposite of this—superficial and shallow. Thump it hard and it will be sure to make a hollow sound. Of course we must also note that much deep thinking is melancholy. From these data we might conclude that deep is doleful and everything cheerful is a superficial waste of time.

The great Hebrew philosopher who wrote this book called Ecclesiastes calls us to joy, but to a joy which *thinks*, a joy which does not shrink back from the hard questions. He calls us to meditation, but to a meditation which does not despair. And as he points out repeatedly, shutting off every avenue of escape, only believers can enjoy the vanity which surrounds us on every side.

## These are the very words of God.
[1]The words of the Preacher, the son of David, king in Jerusalem. [2]Vanity of vanities, saith the Preacher, vanity

of vanities; all is vanity. ³What profit hath a man of all his labour which he taketh under the sun? (Eccl. 1:1–3)

Our author never calls himself Solomon by name, but rather *Qoheleth*. This means *gatherer, assembler,* or *preacher*. Nevertheless, Qoheleth identifies himself here as a son of David, and as a king in Jerusalem. Without entering into a detailed description of the debate between scholars, there is no conclusive reason not to attribute the book to Solomon.

This Solomon was given great wisdom by the Lord, but nevertheless, during the course of his life, he also fell into great enormities. During the time of his apostasy, he introduced the idolatry of some of his foreign wives into the public life of Israel. The book of Ecclesiastes was written in his old age, a repentant rejection of his previous apostasy. Still, that apostasy was grievous and its effects on the generations immediately after Solomon were more lasting than the impact of his repentance.

> But king Solomon loved many strange women, together with the daughter of Pharaoh, women of the Moabites, Ammonites, Edomites, Zidonians, and Hittites; of the nations concerning which the LORD said unto the children of Israel, Ye shall not go in to them, neither shall they come in unto you: for surely they will turn away your heart after their gods: Solomon clave unto these in love. And he had seven hundred wives, princesses, and three hundred concubines: and his wives turned away his heart. For it came to pass, when Solomon was old, that his wives turned away his heart after other gods: and his heart was not perfect with the LORD his God, as was the heart of David his

father. For Solomon went after Ashtoreth the
goddess of the Zidonians, and after Milcom the
abomination of the Ammonites. And Solomon did
evil in the sight of the LORD, and went not fully
after the LORD, as did David his father. Then did
Solomon build an high place for Chemosh, the
abomination of Moab, in the hill that is before
Jerusalem, and for Molech, the abomination of the
children of Ammon. And likewise did he for all
his strange wives, which burnt incense and
sacrificed unto their gods. And the LORD was
angry with Solomon, because his heart was turned
from the LORD God of Israel, which had appeared
unto him twice, and had commanded him concerning this thing, that he should not go after
other gods: but he kept not that which the LORD
commanded.

(1 Kings 11:1–10)

We see the outside of this sin described in the
histories of Scripture. We also see the horrible consequences which afflict Israel in the centuries which follow
Solomon. We see this sin from the inside, and the
repentance following, in the pages of Ecclesiastes. What
did the fall of Solomon—and the fall of Israel—*mean?*
The surprising answer is that it meant nothing—vanity.
Like all sin and unbelief, it came to . . . nothing.

The book demands careful consideration. Unlike the
textual liberal, we should assume a single voice throughout the text of this book. Unlike the pietist, we should
reject the temptation to accept the "edifying" passages
and skim over the apparently difficult ones. And unlike
the heretic, we should reject an elevation of the difficult
texts at the expense of the pervasive orthodoxy of the
book.

Ecclesiastes has four basic sections, or divisions. In the first, Ecclesiastes 1:2–2:26, we see that Solomon's experience shows that satisfaction cannot come from anything within the power or competence of man. In chapters 3:1–5:20, he shows that God is sovereign over *everything*. He then goes on to answer objections to this (perennially offensive) doctrine. Third, Ecclesiastes 6:1–8:15 carefully applies this doctrine that the sovereign God alone gives the power to enjoy this parade of vanity. Without an understanding of the Almighty, and without seeing His attributes, nature, and character, the world is nothing but an ongoing vexation of spirit. And finally, Ecclesiastes 8:16–12:14 removes various obstacles and discouragements, and addresses numerous practical concerns.

Throughout the book, two great refrains can be heard. When we come to understand the meaning of these refrains, we will then know that the meaning of life cannot be found by fumbling in the dark. Instead of viewing the book as a series of disjointed and sometimes contradictory statements, we must first listen for those themes which integrate all the teaching of the entire book. These themes are pervasive throughout all four sections.

The first refrain is summed up in the phrase *under the sun*—the phrase occurs numerous times and is extremely significant. "Under the sun" is the realm where vanity reigns and should be understood as *this* world, considered in its own right. A wise man will always consider and reflect upon what occurs "under the sun." Work has no profit there (1:3; 2:11; 2:22); nothing is really new (1:9); everything is vain (1:14; 4:7); work is distressing (2:17); labor is hateful because someone else

gets the fruit of it (2:18); a fool might receive the
benefit of a man's work (2:19,20); church and state are
together corrupt (3:16); men are oppressed, of course
(4:1); the unborn are at a distinct advantage (4:3);
popularity is in constant flux (4:15); riches destroy their
owners (5:13); the wealthy are unable to enjoy their
wealth (6:1); future generations are unknowable (6:12);
men rule others and destroy themselves (8:9); work is
incomprehensible (8:17); both good and evil men die
(9:3); our emotions perish with us (9:6); time and
chance happen to us all (9:11); ungrateful men despise
the benefits of wisdom (9:13); and rulers establish the
blind folly of egalitarianism (10:5).

All this—and a good deal more fooling about—
occurs under the sun. These persistent reminders
throughout the book are what make Ecclesiastes such a
bane to cheerful fools.

But another theme, another refrain, is equally
marked, and this one is missed by the cynic. This is the
refrain which sings *the great gift of God*. Under the sun,
vanity is God's scepter (5:18; 8:15; 9:9). For those who
fear Him, He gives the gift of being able to actually
enjoy this great big marching band of futility—the tubas
of vanity bringing up the rear. God gives to a wise man
the gift of watching, with a pious and grateful chuckle,
one damn thing after another. All things considered, the
furious activity of this world is about as meaningful as
the half-time frenzy at the Super Bowl. But a wise man
can be there and enjoy himself. *This* is the gift of God.
The wise will notice how this point is hammered home,
throughout the book, again and again. Slowly it dawns
on a man that this is really a book of profound . . .
*optimism*. "I know that nothing is better" (3:12–13); "So

I perceived that nothing is better" (3:22); "Here is what I have seen: It is good and fitting" (5:18–19); "So I commended enjoyment" (8:15); "Go, eat your bread with joy" (9:7–9).

All these things are done by those who fear God under the sun, just as the miserable will constantly sweat and labor under the sun. But the distinction, *as always*, is to be found in the sovereignty and grace of God. This is why the doctrinal foundation for joy—joy that lives at the end of the tether—must first be understood. When he understands, and not until then, a man may eat his bread, drink his wine, and rejoice. He may work hard, digging a hole that another will someday fill up. If he is a wise man, he will know that this work is vain and he will rejoice in it anyway. This is the gift of God. How is it possible? The subject is worth considering.

# The Meaning of Joy

*Judge not according to the appearance, but judge righteous judgment.*
John 7:24

We must guard ourselves. Sincere and thoughtful Christians need to resist two errors of interpretation as they seek to understand this small book of wisdom. The first is that of treating the word *vanity* as modern existentialists would treat it, meaning absolute meaninglessness. Of course, from beginning to end, including Ecclesiastes in the middle, the Bible rejects this error. And further, if Solomon were arguing the absolute meaninglessness of absolutely everything, then why should we trust his argument? It too is under the sun. How could anything, or any word, *mean* utter meaninglessness? Whenever anyone announces that there is no such thing as truth, a listener should always wonder if the speaker believes his expression to be *true*. Solomon is a wiser man than to fall into the idiocy of modern existential relativism. So vanity in this book does not mean final and ultimate absurdity; something else is in view, which we will consider in its place.[1]

But the other error, common among the devout, is

to rush headlong to pious and edifying conclusions before letting the force of Solomon's observations and argument work into our souls. We must not hasten to heal this particular wound lightly. The meaninglessness of all things, as Solomon presents it, must work down into our bones. We should let the Word do its work before we hasten to make Ecclesiastes a grab bag of inspirational quotes. If we are not careful, we will fall into the trap of writing pious drivel, saying that Solomon meant to say down is up instead of down is down. It can be a painful experience to read the work of devout commentators working manfully away as they try to sandpaper the rough spots in Ecclesiastes—it has to be *smooth* to be edifying.

If we want to avoid these pitfalls, we must begin by looking ahead a few pages. The first division of the book (Eccl. 1:2–2:26) can be divided into three sections. We will be considering the first of these subsections shortly (1:4–11). But before addressing these verses, we should look ahead at the conclusion of the first division to see where Solomon's argument is taking us. I have italicized a modification of the AV translation here.[2]

> *There is not a good [inherent] in man* that he should eat and drink, and that his soul should enjoy good in his labor. This also, I saw, was from the hand of God. For who can eat, or who can have enjoyment, *apart from Him?* For God gives wisdom and knowledge and joy to a man who is good in His sight; but to the sinner He gives the work of gathering and collecting, that he may give to him who is good before God. This also is vanity and grasping for the wind.
>
> (Eccl. 2:24–26)

Obviously, we need to begin with the translation issues. In many translations, this section begins with "Nothing is better . . ." Scholars have inserted the word *better* here, even though the Hebrew text does not have it. This is done because that phrase *does* occur several other times in this book and it has simply been assumed that it was dropped out here. As it stands, however, it should be translated, "There is not a good [inherent] in man that he . . ."

Also, verse 25 should not read, "more than I," referring to Solomon, but rather, "apart from Him," referring to God. This is the reading followed by eight Hebrew manuscripts, the Septuagint, the Syriac, the Coptic, and the translation of Jerome into Latin. This is also the reading which fits best within the context of the argument.

So the message here is twofold. God is the One who gives things, and God is the one who gives the power to enjoy things. These are distinct gifts . . . just as a can of peaches and a can-opener are distinct gifts. Only the first is given to the unbeliever. The believer is given both, which is simply another way of saying that he is given the capacity for enjoyment. If we remember that this is the conclusion of this section of Solomon's argument, it can help us understand what he intends as he lays out his premises.

**Blessed are they that keep His testimonies.**
⁴One generation passeth away, and another generation cometh: but the earth abideth for ever. ⁵The sun also ariseth, and the sun goeth down, and hasteth to his place where he arose. ⁶The wind goeth toward the south, and turneth about unto the north; it whirleth about

continually, and the wind returneth again according to his circuits. ⁷All the rivers run into the sea; yet the sea is not full; unto the place from whence the rivers come, thither they return again. ⁸All things are full of labour; man cannot utter it: the eye is not satisfied with seeing, nor the ear filled with hearing.

⁹The thing that hath been, it is that which shall be; and that which is done is that which shall be done: and there is no new thing under the sun. ¹⁰Is there any thing whereof it may be said, See, this is new? it hath been already of old time, which was before us. ¹¹There is no remembrance of former things; neither shall there be any remembrance of things that are to come with those that shall come after. (Eccl. 1:4–11)

As we have considered, vanity does not refer to an absolute meaninglessness. We see now that it refers to *an inscrutable repetitiveness.* You washed the dishes last night, and there they are again. You changed the oil in your car three months ago, and now you are doing it *again.* All is vanity. This shirt was clean yesterday.

Solomon sees that generations come and go—one group of people replaces another (v. 4), and they are not really aware of one another (v. 11). Underneath them the stubborn earth stays put (v. 4). When the history of some group of people who lived previously intrudes upon us, we may be briefly amused or intrigued. But we do not really come to the point where we *learn.* Further, we should have every expectation that those who follow us will act in just the same way toward us. We will slip out of their memories, just as countless generations have slipped out of ours. This happens again and again, over and over. As the fellow said, the only thing we learn from history is that we don't learn from history.

The sun rises, sets, and hustles back to rise again. Like the hypocrite at his prayers, the sun engages in vain repetition. The sun that rose this morning is the same one that Abraham, Odysseus, David, Paul, Voltaire, Isaac Watts, and Robert E. Lee saw. And when the sun goes down, we have every expectation of seeing it again. It does not necessarily expect to see *us* again.

The jet stream runs in circles too—the natural world, it appears, runs in circles. So do we. What goes up comes down. What goes down comes up again. This is the meaning of vanity. Spinning wheels got to go round, as a fellow on the radio put it. A man may look in vain for something new in the weather. Water evaporates, rains, evaporates, and rains again, and the ocean never fills up. This whole world is a gigantic chalkboard illustration for us. Look at it as Solomon did, and learn a wearisome lesson.

We may try to break free of this repetition by saying that it does not exist. We may *ignore* the past and say, "See, *this* is new" (vv. 9–11). The latest "whatever" is whooped as the savior which will lead us out of our temporary postmodern malaise, our deep blue funk. Perhaps the Internet, or computers, or skyscrapers, or environmental activism, or snowboarding, or something will save us. But this does not help. Even the snowboarder, when he gets to the bottom, has to get back up to the top again.

And further, even this error is a repetition. The man who says he has found something new is *being* something old. As sure as the sun rises, men will continue to make the same mistake except for those to whom God gives *wisdom*. Every morning folly comes up over the horizon.

Again. Morning, sunshine. Time to put the coffee on.
Again.

To be wise, a man must know his limitations. "All
things are full of labour; man cannot utter it . . ." (v. 8).
A wise believer is a man who knows the length of his
tether. Only through the wisdom which God gives can he
come to *enjoy* this limitation, this restriction, this vanity.
And while a wise man may come to enjoy this vanity,
even he cannot really express it.

# A Taste of Nothing

*For what profit is it to a man if he gains the whole world, and loses his own soul? Or what will a man give in exchange for his soul?*
Matthew 16:26

The theory is plain by our own lights; we see nothing around us but inscrutable repetition. But Solomon's experience is provided to us here in order to give us a better understanding of our world as a revolving emptyset.

## O that my ways were directed to keep thy statutes!

[12]I the Preacher was king over Israel in Jerusalem. [13]And I gave my heart to seek and search out by wisdom concerning all things that are done under heaven: this sore travail hath God given to the sons of man to be exercised therewith. [14]I have seen all the works that are done under the sun; and, behold, all is vanity and vexation of spirit. [15]That which is crooked cannot be made straight: and that which is wanting cannot be numbered. [16]I communed with mine own heart, saying, Lo, I am come to great estate, and have gotten more wisdom than all they

that have been before me in Jerusalem: yea, my heart had great experience of wisdom and knowledge. [17]And I gave my heart to know wisdom, and to know madness and folly: I perceived that this also is vexation of spirit. [18]For in much wisdom is much grief: and he that increaseth knowledge increaseth sorrow. (Eccl. 1:12–18)

The descent into hell begins. Solomon had set himself to a particular task, that of figuring it all out (1:12–18). He set his heart to seek (v. 13), and he communed with his heart on the subject (v. 16). He set his heart to *know* (v. 17). This is his testimony of his descent into madness and folly. He fell away from God with his eyes open, looking around himself the while. The whole investigation was a sorry business, producing sorry results.

The fool sets about straightening the crooked. But Solomon, eyes open, saw that the crooked cannot be straightened out (1:15). And why not? Looking ahead, we see that it is because *God* is the one who made it crooked (7:13). This burdensome task is therefore God's doing (1:13). There is a purpose behind this meaninglessness—it is the purpose and intent of God that sinners cannot straighten what *He* has made crooked.

A popular notion is about, that God is above all this crooked mess down here, wringing His hands over a world gone bad. Whenever some public calamity befalls us, some soupy minister is bound to get some air time, assuring all that "God's heart was the first to break." This "let's-keep-God-away-from-responsibility-for-the-bad-stuff" theology seeks, in a superficial way, to defend the honor of God. If God is not really here, then we cannot blame Him for the problem of evil.[1] And so we

reason to ourselves, thinking that man by his free will has
made something crooked which God cannot, for various
reasons, straighten out. The problem with this idea is
that Solomon states it the other way. Man cannot
straighten what *God* has made crooked. Contrary to our
modern evangelical apostles of uplift, *God* has given us
"sore travail" (v. 13).

We like to think that God does not "do" earthquakes. We assure an unbelieving world that we do not
serve a God who wields natural disasters or any other
kind of disaster. We have only one tiny problem with the
thesis. "Shall there be evil in a city, and the Lord hath
not done it?" (Amos 3:6).

Of course, wisdom is a pain in the neck. Within
these boundaries, wisdom can only show that God has
determined to trap us in a meaningless existence. So any
intelligent investigation of the world and its pleasures
will only multiply sorrows (1:18). The fool thinks he is
chained to a dungeon wall; the intelligent knows that it is
actually a labyrinth. Pleasures, delights, sensations, and
all their cousins, will only send a man, first on this fool's
errand, and then on that one.

**Blessed art thou, O Lord: teach me thy statutes.**
¹I said in mine heart, Go to now, I will prove thee with
mirth, therefore enjoy pleasure: and, behold, this also is
vanity. ²I said of laughter, It is mad: and of mirth, What
doeth it? (Eccl. 2:1–2)

He comes first to this thing and then to that.
Solomon had chosen a disciplined pursuit of meaning
under the sun, *apart* from God's blessing and gift. Using
his intelligence and wisdom, he sought to plumb the

depths of madness and all folly. Maybe some kind of an
answer can be found *there* (1:17). So his wisdom sought
out various devices.

The first device was laughter. Perhaps the solution
to the problem presented by this cycling world can be
found in comedy. Maybe the world would be a cheerier
place if we could add a laugh track to it. Without the
intelligence and wisdom of Solomon, we are trying the
same thing in our day. Perhaps we may find a savior in
comedy. But the ubiquitous laugh track behind all our
sitcoms provides a fitting commentary for our times—it
is nothing but a great comedic cattle prod, which consid-
erately tells the herd when it is supposed to overflow in
jovial mooing. Time to laugh, says our invisible master.

But the laughter is empty and the jokes necessarily
hollow. Those who joke with us either don't know the
situation under the sun, in which case they are stupid, or
they *do* know how bleak everything is, in which case they
are not very funny. *Humor under the sun can only keep its sense
of . . . humor . . . through a blind foolishness.*

**I have rejoiced in the way of thy testimonies.**
³I sought in mine heart to give myself unto wine, yet
acquainting mine heart with wisdom; and to lay hold on
folly, till I might see what was that good for the sons of
men, which they should do under the heaven all the days
of their life. (Eccl. 2:3)

Perhaps a bottle of wine might do the trick. Try two
bottles. Nope (2:3). If this particular anodyne were
taken away, our entire country music industry would
collapse. Shortly after the Fall, men figured out how to
forget their troubles by seeking a pleasant buzz between

their ears. Sometimes the buzz came from grapes, sometimes from grain, and, in other instances, from various kinds of vegetation.

For various reasons it is hard for American Christians to sympathize with this. The first reason is that they do not really understand the problem as Ecclesiastes presents it. When a thinking man looks around at this world as it is, he *should* see that everybody must get stoned. When it is all over, he also sees that it didn't do any good, but, as Solomon shows us, it was an understandable thing to try. The line of reasoning commended itself to the apostle Paul. If Christ did not rise from the dead, then the most sensible thing to do is eat and drink and have as good a time as a meaningless bit of protoplasm can have. If the only thing being considered is what we see here under the sun, then it does not make sense to rally to the defense of traditional values.

The second reason is that we have a hard time understanding the difference between a sin and a crime. Americans are naturally meddlesome. If something is disapproved of, *i.e.*, thought to be sinful, the next step taken is the assertion that "there ought to be a law." Of course others make the facile assumption that since whatever it is should not be a crime, then whatever it is must not be a sin either.

Before addressing Solomon's point about the emptiness of the buzz, please permit a few controversial asides. There should be no war on drugs, and drugs should not be illegal. Cocaine should be readily available at Payless or Safeway—and if we have learned the lessons of Ecclesiastes, we will stock it in the idiot section. But a man will search the Bible in vain for any hint that God wants civil penalties attached to drug use, *per se*. Every other teenager could be getting high like the birds, and this datum would remain none of the civil magistrate's business. It is simply a question of whether this kind of thing ought to be a crime.

Solomon shows us that wine as a mental anesthetic is fruitless. It simply does not work. The same goes for every other thing which a man might use for the same numbing purpose. This is why a wise man like Solomon found no contentment there. Like all sin, it comes up empty.

Drunkenness is of course as empty as the bottle afterwards. The New Testament puts drug use in the same class—hollow. The word is *pharmakeia*, from which we get our word *pharmacy*, and our standard translations are sometimes *odd*. For example, in Galatians 5:20, it is usually rendered as *sorcery* or *witchcraft*. But Thayers gives the first definition as "the use or the administering of drugs." The second definition is *poisoning*, and the third *witchcraft*. Liddell and Scott do much the same. First, it is the use of "drugs, potions, spells." The second definition is *poisoning* or *witchcraft*.

There is a connection to sorcery, but that connection is through the drugs. In biblical times, occult activity was usually drug-related occult activity. Going from English to Greek, if we were to ask what Greek word would describe the practices of our modern-day sky pilots, the answer would be *pharmakeia*.

We may also reason by analogy. Drug use is excluded because it is designed to bring about the one state—brain fog—which is condemned as a lawless application of alcohol.[2] "And be not drunk with wine, wherein is excess; but be filled with the Spirit" (Eph. 5:18). Alcohol has at least five lawful scriptural

uses: the sacramental (Matt. 26:27–28), celebratory
(Ps. 104:15), medicinal (1 Tim. 5:23), aesthetic
(John 2:10), and thirst (John 19:28–30). Of these, the
only lawful use for drugs is the medicinal—and the use
to which everyone puts drugs is the one use denied to
alcohol.

Although drug use has only one lawful use, when
taken in unlawful ways it may still be used in the hands
of a sovereign God to show a man how useless his life is.
The pursuit of wine by Solomon in this section brought
him exactly to this point. In our day, the same thing
commonly happens. Many have sought to figure out
some kind of meaning for life through the ingestion of
various substances. Whether this better-living-through-
chemistry approach comes through liquid, smoke, needle,
or straw, the result is always a vacuum. A fool will always
find various ways to dig his way down, but when he gets
there he is always at the bottom of a hole.

Other epicurean delights figure into this as well.
Obviously, royal feasting was probably connected with
this seeking of meaning in dining pleasure—notice 1
Kings 4:22–23.

> [22]And Solomon's provision for one day was thirty
> measures of fine flour, and threescore measures of
> meal, [23]Ten fat oxen, and twenty oxen out of the
> pastures, and an hundred sheep, beside harts, and
> roebucks, and fallowdeer, and fatted fowl.

It would take about 35,000 people to consume all
of this. Solomon's allotment was considerable, and
impressive. Perhaps meaning can be found here. Eat and
drink, eat and drink, madness and folly. The answer is
always the same—*no.*

Just like wine, food is a creature. Later in our study we will come to the celebratory function in both, but for now we see that good food, good coffee, and good wine are all headed toward the same place, which in most cases is the sewage treatment plant. As a substitute for transcendent meaning, food performs just as poorly as wine. And yet, in every culture flailing after meaning, snobbery with regard to the best restaurants is always a key player.

### I will meditate in thy precepts.

[4]I made me great works; I builded me houses; I planted me vineyards: [5]I made me gardens and orchards, and I planted trees in them of all kind of fruits: [6]I made me pools of water, to water therewith the wood that bringeth forth trees: [7]I got me servants and maidens, and had servants born in my house; also I had great possessions of great and small cattle above all that were in Jerusalem before me. (Eccl. 2:4–7)

Solomon also sought meaning through some great accomplishments—"I made me great works . . ." Solomon built houses, vineyards, gardens, orchards, and water pools; he had servants, herds, silver, and gold. Some of these works of Solomon can still be seen today for those tourists who want to admire an Ozymandian ruin. But when all the monuments have been built, and all the impressive work accomplished, only a fool does not see the emptiness. Ambrose Bierce once pointedly defined a mausoleum as the final and funniest folly of the rich. Shebna used to be a somebody, and built a great tomb to prove it (Is. 22:15–19). We have even found a portion of the lintel from that tomb. *Whoa!* and, *Big deal!*

But this pursuit of meaning in pleasure does not

necessitate a frat-boy ethic. A man might be a hedonist, looking for ultimate meaning and value in aesthetic pleasures that are *not* gross or ostentatious. Perhaps meaning can be found by walking in a groomed Japanese garden contemplating chess moves or geometry problems. While it is certainly more refined, still the results come up the same—and empty every time.

Today such a man, committed to building projects as he was, would be lauded for his "public spirit" and dedication to "public service." But at the end of the day all he has done is build hollow buildings for all the hollow people to live in.

### I will delight myself in thy statutes.

[8]I gathered me also silver and gold, and the peculiar treasure of kings and of the provinces: I gat me men singers and women singers, and the delights of the sons of men, as musical instruments, and that of all sorts. (Eccl. 2:8)

This is groping for meaning in the cultivation of refinement, the aesthetic impulse. Solomon acquired male and female musicians, and every kind of instrument (2:8). These court musicians were no doubt pretty good at what they did. But when they were done, it was in fact *done* and the room filled up with a silent emptiness again. We in our day have tried to solve that problem by refusing to allow silence anywhere, but silence can still intrude at inconvenient times. But we labor manfully onward. We surround ourselves with pleasant noises at all times. At one time, only kings could afford to have the musicians along in order to provide that beautiful background noise, but now, thanks to technology, we can tote it everywhere. We can get that music into every empty space imaginable. We seek peace through eliminating the very idea of a moment's peace.

Solomon's taste was refined—he obtained talented musicians. Our tastes are not as refined—we obtain car stereo systems which can rattle our bones loose with a thumping bass. But in either case, meaning and purpose are not an acoustical matter.

Someone with refined sensibilities may sniff at the mindlessness of pop music, and the kid who thrives on the stuff may roll his adolescent eyes at the very thought of highbrow music. But all of it is useless, slip sliding away.

### I will not forget thy word.

⁹So I was great, and increased more than all that were before me in Jerusalem: also my wisdom remained with me. ¹⁰And whatsoever mine eyes desired I kept not from them, I withheld not my heart from any joy; for my heart rejoiced in all my labour: and this was my portion of all my labour. ¹¹Then I looked on all the works that my hands had wrought, and on the labour that I had laboured to do: and, behold, all was vanity and vexation of spirit, and there was no profit under the sun. (Eccl. 2:9–11)

So Solomon grew great and that same Solomon began to flail. He sought out *any* pleasure—Did he leave anything undone? Not really. Solomon said that if it felt good, he did it (2:10). He indulged in every conceivable kick that a king in his position might desire. The chances are good that Solomon gave way to every vice. But nothing good came from it. When a lawful pleasure is indulged apart from God's gift, nothing good can come from it. And when unlawful pleasures are permitted by God, He never gives satisfaction with it. In either case, the only thing left is the stain on the conscience and the entry of the sin in God's ledger. The entry, as always, amounts to zero.

Think for a moment of what Solomon was in a position to do. We should meditate briefly on what he probably did. He had a thousand women, all of them built from the ground up, and all good-looking. He had more money than a man can spend. He had vast estates. He had time to pursue every possible kick in every possible corner of his palaces.

But it was all a bunch of nothing. "And I looked . . ." When Solomon was done, he saw that he had no profit. And as we pursue the same things, neither do we. This road has been traveled before. When we get to the end, the road just stops, with barely room for the car to turn around.

## Overview and Review

First division (1:2–2:26): Satisfaction cannot come from anything within man's power. This point can be confirmed in two places, settled in two ways. First subdivision (1:2–1:11): Nature shows an inscrutable repetition. Second subdivision (1:12–2:11): Empty experience shows Solomon that experience is empty.

Second division (3:1–5:20): God is sovereign over everything that is. Everyone who holds this doctrine has always had to answer objections to it, and Solomon is no different.

Third division (6:1–8:15): Doctrine is always meant for application and so Solomon applies his doctrine that it is the sovereign God alone who gives the power to enjoy vanity.

Fourth division (8:16–12:14): The last section removes various obstacles and discouragements and addresses practical concerns.

# The End of the Tether

*For what shall it profit a man, if he shall gain the whole world, and lose his own soul?*

Mark 8:36

Courtesy of ancient Rome, one epitaph sums the situation up quite nicely: "Bathing, wine, and love-affairs—these hurt our bodies, but they make life worth living. I've lived my days. I revelled, and I drank all that I desired. Once I was not; then I was; now I am not again but I don't care!" On the edge of the abyss, we see a defiant yell from another insightful fool. But even an insightful fool cannot see very far.

**I will keep thy statutes: O forsake me not utterly.** [12]And I turned myself to behold wisdom, and madness, and folly: for what can the man do that cometh after the king? even that which hath been already done. [13]Then I saw that wisdom excelleth folly, as far as light excelleth darkness. [14]The wise man's eyes are in his head; but the fool walketh in darkness: and I myself perceived also that one event happeneth to them all. [15]Then said I in my heart, As it happeneth to the fool, so it happeneth even to me; and why was I then more wise? Then I said in my heart, that this also is vanity. [16]For there is no remembrance of the wise more than of the fool for ever; seeing that which now is in the days to come shall all be forgotten. And how dieth the wise man? as the fool. (Eccl. 2:12–16)

Consider the results of the experiment thus far. Solomon has already seen that the sky is impenetrable. He then turned and experimented with everything he could eat, drink, smoke, or sleep with, and has found that meaning is not to be found there. So now he *turns* (v. 12) and looks back over the ground he has traveled.

This leads him to affirm the obvious. We can see that even in this experience of sin Solomon has not become a relativist. Despite the meaninglessness, Solomon sees that wisdom is still better than folly. Better to go over a cliff with eyes open than with eyes shut. Better, as the fellow said, to be Socrates dissatisfied than a pig satisfied. Every thinking man instinctively feels that this is the better choice, but defending that choice under the sun is a dicier matter. Why would we be repulsed if someone offered to turn us into an especially contented moo cow? Or a very happy mud turtle?

But both the fool and the wise man have the same destination. Although wisdom is better, Solomon cannot yet tell us *why* it is better. From what happens to the wise man and fool *here*, under the sun, the results figure to be about the same. Both kinds of men die. They both are buried. They both rot. However, a difference can be noted. The wise man has eyes in his head, and the fool is blind. And yet still they both die (v. 16). So whether this difference makes a difference, we shall see. Redemption

cannot even be found in posthumous reputation (v. 16).
Wisdom *under the sun* stops breathing at some point just
like folly does (vv. 14–16). In this respect, the wise man,
no less than the fool, will at some point quietly assume
room temperature.

Solomon knows that the position of the wise man is
better, but he cannot say why. All the data under the sun
that he can find shows that the wise and foolish wind up
in the same graveyard. So Solomon expresses his preference for wisdom, a preference suspended, in good
Kantian fashion, in mid-air. The categorical imperative,
that imperial voice from the void, must be obeyed. At the
same time, the wise man is disgusted that he has no *reason*
for trusting his reason, no wisdom as the foundation for
his wisdom.

### Hide not thy commandments from me.

[17]Therefore I hated life; because the work that is wrought
under the sun is grievous unto me: for all is vanity and
vexation of spirit. [18]Yea, I hated all my labour which I
had taken under the sun: because I should leave it unto
the man that shall be after me. [19]And who knoweth
whether he shall be a wise man or a fool? yet shall he
have rule over all my labour wherein I have laboured, and
wherein I have shewed myself wise under the sun. This is
also vanity. [20]Therefore I went about to cause my heart
to despair of all the labour which I took under the sun.
[21]For there is a man whose labour is in wisdom, and in
knowledge, and in equity; yet to a man that hath not
laboured therein shall he leave it for his portion. This
also is vanity and a great evil. [22]For what hath man of all
his labour, and of the vexation of his heart, wherein he
hath laboured under the sun? [23]For all his days are

sorrows, and his travail grief; yea, his heart taketh not rest in the night. This is also vanity. (Eccl. 2:17–23)

This provokes Solomon, and so he comes to say that he couldn't care less.† "Therefore I hated life" (v. 17). This is meaninglessness *prior to the gift of God* which makes it enjoyable. The word for *hate* here includes the idea of *contempt* or *disdain*. He really couldn't care less. Solomon is preparing the way for us to come to a great truth. The gift of God does not make this meaninglessness go away; the gift of God makes this vanity enjoyable.

But in the meantime, Look, we are told, at the boneheads to come. Because the wise die, they must leave what they have done to others. And will *they* be wise? Who knows? The result is distress (v. 17), despair (v. 20), sorrow (v. 23), burdens (v. 23), and restlessness (v. 23). Solomon *turns his heart* to this despair (v. 20). He despairs of any way out under the sun. Just as he gave himself to pleasure before, so now he gives way to despair.

### Thy servant did meditate in thy statutes.
²⁴There is nothing better for a man, than that he should eat and drink, and that he should make his soul enjoy good in his labour. This also I saw, that it was from the hand of God. ²⁵For who can eat, or who else can hasten hereunto, more than I? ²⁶For God giveth to a man that is good in his sight wisdom, and knowledge, and joy: but to the sinner he giveth travail, to gather and to heap up, that he may give to him that is good before God. This also is vanity and vexation of spirit. (Eccl. 2:24–26)

This is the conclusion to the first portion of
Solomon's argument. Solomon's wisdom under the sun,
and all his experiments, have brought him to an impasse.
But an impasse for men is not an impasse for God. So
what is the conclusion? Remember the translation
discussion on this section earlier in the book.

> *There is not a good [inherent] in man* that he should eat
> and drink, and that his soul should enjoy good in
> his labor. This also, I saw, was from the hand of
> God. For who can eat, or who can have enjoyment,
> *apart from Him?* For God gives wisdom and
> knowledge and joy to a man who is good in His
> sight; but to the sinner He gives the work of
> gathering and collecting, that he may give to him
> who is good before God. This also is vanity and
> grasping for the wind.
>
> (Eccl. 2:24–26)

Man cannot be thought of as an artesian well.
Nothing inherent in him enables him to enjoy his
creature comforts. He has no innate capacity to enjoy.
Further, this is God's doing—*God* is the one who has
imposed this inexorable law upon us (vv. 24–25). Who
can enjoy even his food apart from God?

God always dispenses His gifts with a sovereign
and majestic grace. The gifts are wisdom and knowledge
and joy. Wisdom is grace, and knowledge is also grace,
but note particularly the last of these—*joy.* Joy is a
crowning gift of God in this meaningless world. The
seraphim experience joy in the presence of God, but
honestly, that is to be expected. It is not the angels He
helps. We are given the privilege of experiencing joy *here,*
in the midst of ongoing disobedient and imbecilic chaos.

Joy, yes, but *mirabile dictu*, the joy is *here*.

In the meantime, what is the job of the sinner? He is called upon to accumulate loads of stuff, to rake those good things into heaps and piles . . . which only the godly may enjoy.

And who will inherit all these worldly goods? Just a few verses earlier, this question could not be answered. Prior to the gift of God, who knows whether the fool will inherit the goods of the wise? According to *our* lights, who can tell whether a wise man or a fool will inherit? But according to faith, the answer is now plain—those who are good before God. The wicked are left to their vexations.

In one of his songs, Bob Seeger says there are two holes in the head where the light is *supposed* to get by. And so, does it? How can an unexamined piety differ from the blind gropings of the fool? What is the hallmark of wisdom in this fallen world? The answer is *joy* at the end of the tether. But before we can learn joy at the end of the tether, we must learn the strength of that tether. The Lord is God and we are not.

### Overview and Review

First division (1:2–2:26): Satisfaction cannot be coaxed from any created thing by man's power or cunning. First subdivision (1:2–1:11): Nature repeats herself, again and again, for no reason in particular that *we* can see. Second subdivision (1:12–2:11): Solomon knows through hard experience that sensation is empty. Third subdivision (2:12–2:26): Wisdom is better, but only God knows why. God gives a wondrous gift, which is joy chained to a wall.

Second division (3:1–5:20): Everyone wants God

to be sovereign. No one appears to want Him sovereign in everything and over everything. Solomon insists on it anyway and answers objections to the doctrine.

Third division (6:1–8:15): Because God is sovereign in all things, He has the power to give enjoyment down here. So Solomon applies his doctrine that the sovereign God alone gives the power to enjoy vanity.

Fourth division (8:16–12:14): At the last, Solomon turns, as all good teachers must, to remove various obstacles and discouragements, and to address practical concerns.

# Beautiful in Its Time

*If there is calamity in a city, will not the LORD have done it?*
Amos 3:6

A common illustration of the ways of God and the
understanding of man is that of a tapestry on a loom.
From the vantage underneath, little is visible but snarls
and knots. But above, the beautiful pattern of the work
on the loom can be seen. As Solomon has shown, we live
out our lives under the loom, and everything we see is
vanity. So how can we see the pattern above? The only
possible answer is through faith in the sovereign God.

**O let me not wander from thy commandments.**
[1]To every thing there is a season, and a time to every
purpose under the heaven: [2]A time to be born, and a time
to die; a time to plant, and a time to pluck up that which
is planted; [3]A time to kill, and a time to heal; a time to
break down, and a time to build up; [4]A time to weep, and
a time to laugh; a time to mourn, and a time to dance; [5]A
time to cast away stones, and a time to gather stones
together; a time to embrace, and a time to refrain from
embracing; [6]A time to get, and a time to lose; a time to

keep, and a time to cast away; ⁷A time to rend, and a time
to sew; a time to keep silence, and a time to speak; ⁸A
time to love, and a time to hate; a time of war, and a time
of peace. ⁹What profit hath he that worketh in that
wherein he laboureth? ¹⁰I have seen the travail, which
God hath given to the sons of men to be exercised in it.
(Eccl. 3:1–10)

Despite the misfortune of having been made famous
by the Byrds, this passage remains a great expression of
the way men live their lives before the Lord.

We have now begun the second section of
Solomon's argument, and so we should again look ahead
at his conclusion to this second stage of the argument.
We must continue to keep our eyes where we are going.
"Here is what I have seen: It is good and fitting for one
to eat and drink . . ." (Eccl. 5:18–20). The reader must
never forget that this is a book of exuberant, fierce, and
hard driving joy. When Solomon arrives at his conclusions of joy, this is not because he is taking an existen-
tialist leap into the dark. He is not pulling an elephant
out of a hat. What he says *follows* from his premises.

The basis for this joy is the principle of divine
sovereignty. Now the days of our lives are in the hands
of God. The first verse here says that there is a time and
season for *everything* under heaven (v. 1). So who apportions these times and seasons? All these tasks which
follow are God-given (v. 10); *He* makes everything
beautiful in its time (v. 11); God's inscrutable actions
(v. 11) are forever (v. 14). If it is good, then God gave
it. If it is travail, then God gave it also. In short, He is
the one who apportions our lot, and when He has done
it, it is *forever*. When looked at from our vantage under

the sun, everything (including the ebb and flow) is vanity. But when we remember that God has placed all things where they now are, everything (including the ebb and flow) is *beautiful* (v. 11). A careful reader looks ahead to verse 14. God does all this that men should *fear*. A man who reads without trembling has forgotten the living God.

So this famous passage does *not* contain marching orders for us. It is no agenda. Rather, this is a description of *God's* determinations. We are not being told that it is time to sow now, and a few months later, that it is time for us to hustle up, to get out there and reap. We are being told that we have been placed in a world that we did not create or fashion, and that this world has various repetitive cycles, to which cycles we have been assigned by someone else. We are under the authority of these repetitions and have been placed under that authority by the hand and purpose of God.

Of course, there is a time to be born and a time to die. Who sets these times? Who dictated and arranged for his own birth day? God appoints our birth day and our funeral day (v. 2). No one, before he is born, can be found sitting at some table in the spiritual realm requesting his life. No one asked for their first birth day—it was thrust upon each of us. This wisdom is as neglected as it is obvious. "Seeing his days are determined, the number of his months are with thee, thou hast appointed his bounds that he cannot pass" (Job 14:5). If someone were to show Solomon a man whose days were *not* determined, he would marvel at the prodigy and wonder if the presenter were still back in chapter one, drinking too much wine.

But God is not just concerned with man. His

sovereignty extends to everything and over everything. As our Lord Jesus taught, it includes the hairs of our heads and the birds on our lawn being stalked by the neighbor's cat. Solomon here shows that the lifespan of plants in the field is determined by God. There is a time to plant and a time to harvest. God appoints the birth day of every plant and the funeral of every plant (v. 2). Because this doctrine stinks in our nostrils, we are apt to study arguments to find a way out. But God only promised a way of escape from every temptation, not from every unpalatable doctrine. "Are not two sparrows sold for a farthing? and one of them shall not fall on the ground without your Father. But the very hairs of your head are all numbered" (Matt. 10:29–30). We do not harvest in spring, and we do not sow in winter. We do not do these things, because God has appointed the way it goes.

We see killing times and healing times. These, too, come from the hand of God. God oversees when men are executed or when they are slaughtered in battle. He determines when men are lifted up and restored (v. 3). Who can say that his life ended because God glanced away for a moment? When men are thrust into the maw and grind of war, the fools among them think they are shaping their own destiny. But every arrow, every bullet, follows the path ordained for it before the worlds were made. King Ahab thought he could thwart the words of God by putting on a different set of clothes—as though God would be squinting at the battle from a distance. But an arrow by chance struck him at the joint of his armor, and not a word of the prophet fell to the ground (1 Kings 22: 28, 34). Man is at his most proud in times of war. He vaunts himself because he has beaten his enemy—or thinks he can. But we do not control our destinies in war. God is the one who brings war, and God brings peace again (v. 8).

Times come in which men break down and destroy, followed by times in which they build up again. When either happens, God is there. If it is broken, then God was in the breaking of it. If it is built up, then the Lord was in the building (v. 3). "The counsel of the Lord standeth for ever, the thoughts of his heart to all generations" (Ps. 33:11). Men may boast in what they build, or in what they tear down, but in either case, the Lord stands behind them, wielding them as the instrument of His powerful hands. Does Assyria boast in her power to destroy Israel? The Lord was the one who swung the axe (Is. 10:15). Does a man boast in his ability to go to another city and make a fortune there? He ought to say that the result depends upon the will of God (James 4:13–17).

A time comes to weep; a time comes around when we laugh. Our tears of grief, and the occasions of them, are from His hand. So is the laughter (v. 4). "I am the Lord, and there is none else. I form the light, and create darkness: I make peace, and create evil: I the Lord do all these things" (Is. 45:6b–7). When calamity comes, and the tears follow, the Lord was in it. When rejoicing brings relief, the Lord was in it. This doctrine has a hard edge and more than one person has cut himself on it. But denial of the doctrine does not remove the light and darkness, the peace or evil. It just removes the possibility of finding any solace.

Chesterton once commented that if it is true that a man can find pleasure in skinning a cat, then we must either deny that there is a God, as the atheist does, or deny fellowship between God and man, as the Christian does. He commented further that the new theologians think it an adequate solution to deny the cat. In a comparable way, calamity and evil confront us in the world as brute facts. Those who want to keep the God of the Bible, and yet pretend He is not sovereign over all such things are just not paying attention, either to the argument or to their newspapers. The problem of evil is one which torments urbane thinkers in philosophy departments around the world. I suggest that some hardy believer, at the next faculty dinner, should rise and propose a toast—to the problem of evil. There will be a great blessing in it.

Not surprisingly, this means that mourning is from His will. He appoints the time of mourning. Some time elapses, and He then appoints dancing (v. 4). When a man's soul is cast down, he may turn to the Lord with his lament. "For I have eaten ashes like bread, and mingled my drink with weeping, because of thine indignation and thy wrath: for thou hast lifted me up, and cast me down. My days are like a shadow that declineth; and I am withered like grass" (Ps. 102:9–11). And when the prayer is answered, his gladness may also be attributed to the goodness of the One who gave it. "To appoint unto them that mourn in Zion, to give unto them beauty for ashes, the oil of joy for mourning, the garment of praise for the spirit of heaviness; that they might be called trees of righteousness, the planting of the Lord, that he might be glorified" (Is. 61:3). We tear our clothes in grief. This is from the Lord. We sew in order to clothe ourselves again. The grief is His gift, and so is the restoration (v. 7).

Sometimes we cast stones, and other times we gather them. God gives the time of demolition; He gives the time of construction (v. 5). When a building falls, whether through man's intention or not, the Lord has appointed the time. All construction is futile apart from His good purpose. "Except the Lord build the house, they labour in vain that build it: except the Lord keep the city, the watchman waketh but in vain" (Ps. 127:1).

Holding one another is from Him. An embrace is given from heaven. Abstinence is from Him also. When we refrain from embracing we are fulfilling His appointed will (v. 5). A prudent wife is from the Lord— and so is an attractive one. When we hold each other, we are receiving a gracious gift. When a rift develops, we are still under His decree.

Some people make a lot of money, living in a time for gain. Others lose a great deal. Prosperity is His gift, and so are stock-market crashes (v. 6). God allows us to store it all up. He appoints the day we throw it away, not caring about it any more (v. 6). God is the one who gives the power to get wealth (Dt. 8:18). And when men forget Him, He is the one who brings financial calamity upon them. "Cursed shall be thy basket and thy store"(Dt. 28:17). The commotion of the stock market reveals the hubris of man better than few other things. We believe we can pump up the Dow forever and make money at a fine clip forever . . . but we cannot. The cycles ordained by God for everything in this fallen and silly world will come around again, and many a millionaire will go white in disbelief. "How could this happen?" Friend, look at the world. How could it *not*?

God enables a man to say nothing, keeping his silence. God gives him words to speak (v. 7). "The preparations of the heart in man, and the answer of the tongue, is from the Lord" (Prov. 16:1). The man may think he knows the import of what he says, but only the Lord really understands the direction of the words. Silence and eloquence are both bestowed by Him—and to fulfill His good purpose and will.

Relationships which form are under His sovereign will, and relationships which dissolve are all from Him as well (v. 8). Euodia and Syntyche once were close and had a falling out. No longer under the sun, they are together again. The time for the friendships and the time for the quarrels are all appointed. Our responsibility to avoid foolish quarrels in no way threatens the Lord's sovereignty over our obedience—and our disobedience. We like to argue against these obvious truths because we think it threatens the holiness of God's character to say that God is over all. But remember, He is *God*.

In all this, in every aspect of our lives, the Lord God is exhaustively sovereign. This is not said in order to quarrel with those unhappy brethren who dispute it. This is said because it is the foundation of Solomon's argument, which in turn means that it is the foundation of all possible intelligent joy.

### Thy testimonies are my delight and my counsellors.

[11]He hath made every thing beautiful in his time: also he hath set the world in their heart, so that no man can find out the work that God maketh from the beginning to the end. [12]I know that there is no good in them, but for a man to rejoice, and to do good in his life. [13]And also that every man should eat and drink, and enjoy the good of all his labour, it is the gift of God. [14]I know that, whatsoever God doeth, it shall be for ever: nothing can be put to it, nor any thing taken from it: and God doeth it, that

men should fear before him. <sup>15</sup>That which hath been is now; and that which is to be hath already been; and God requireth that which is past. (Eccl. 3:11–3:15)

Eternity has been placed in our hearts. God has made us in relation to Him, and nothing we can do will alter this. He is always our Maker and we are always made. He is always Creator and we are always created. The fact that the "world" has been placed in our hearts does not mean that we understand the world. The reality is quite the reverse. No man can find out the work which God does from the beginning and to the end. The believing response is to throw up one's hands in faith (not despair) and have a good time. This cannot happen unless one of the works God is doing is the impartation of true faith to another poor sap under the sun.

Now Solomon by faith has seen the profit in things, and the God-given task (v. 9). What He has done is *beautiful* in its time (v. 11). Why do we want to figure it all out? God has placed eternity in our hearts (v. 11), which gives us a desperate thirst without water. But even with this thirst for the eternal, man is not the starting point of knowledge and cannot be. We must begin with *God* and not just any old divinity. We must begin with the God who rules all things, the One who places every-thing in a beautiful place. We must worship the One who orients all things to His ultimate glory. Even sin and evil? Even the monstrous and the ugly? The answer must be *yes*—we are called to remember the list which wisdom gives includes healing and killing, war and hate, mourn-ing and laughter. God controls it all *perfectly*.

We buck when we hear these things because we are proud. We say that we do not want God's holiness impugned, but really we do not want our autonomy restricted. If God appoints all the seasons of every man's life, then no man can live unto himself, and no man can find the fount of wisdom within. If God decrees all things, then I cannot escape Him, not even by plunging myself into all depravity. A man who embraces evil simply finds himself a tool in the hand of the Almighty. A man who rejects evil and follows wisdom finds himself a son in the family of the Almighty. The one option not offered us is that of thwarting and restricting the purposes of God.

Those who say that a holy God cannot wield a wicked tool have come to believe the authority of their own sophistries. The Bible tells us that God is *holy*, and the Bible tells us that God wields the wicked in His hand like an ax. God used the wicked Assyrians to judge the Jews; God used Herod, Pontius Pilate, and all the Jews to condemn His Son; God used Judas to betray the Lord; God used Absalom to sleep with David's concubines. The list is much longer and much less pleasant than many Christians want.

What should we then do? This doctrine is the *foundation* of joy. Rejoice, do good, eat your bread, drink your wine. Believe in the sovereign God and enjoy these inscrutable repetitions (v. 15). This is His gift (v. 13). Remember His judgments (v. 15) and sit down to your dinner.

### Overview and Review
First division (1:2–2:26): Of course satisfaction cannot come from anything within man's power; we can know this from watching the weather channel and by watching our own lives go round and round.

Second division (3:1–5:20): God is sovereign over everything; Solomon answers objections to the doctrine. First subdivision (3:1–3:15): God in His sovereignty places everything in a beautiful place with a perfect and unerring eye.

Third division (6:1–8:15): Solomon follows the scriptural pattern and applies his doctrine that the sovereign God alone gives the power to enjoy vanity.

Fourth division (8:16–12:14): The last section addresses and removes various problems, obstacles, and discouragements, and pointedly comes to practical concerns.

# The Silence of Despair

*If in this life only we have hope in Christ, we are of all men most
miserable.*

I Corinthians 15:19

In considering the book of Ecclesiastes, the question is
not really how to keep the book from contradicting other
portions of more "respectable" Scripture. The task is to
read it in such a way that it does not contradict *itself*. We
are coming to portions of the book which are commonly
misunderstood because readers try to make them stand
on their own, by themselves, and not as part of the
sustained argument.

To understand this argument we have to remember
the nature of hard questions. A wise man will always
recall the boundaries which have been set by Solomon
through the course of the book and the conclusions
throughout the book which *he* urges the reader to draw.
These conclusions are not the same as those which we
would come to if left to our own devices. If left to our
own fleshly wisdom, we would not reason from his
premises the way he does. In this section we again see
Solomon's *odd* kind of conclusion, this time in 3:22.

"Wherefore I perceive that there is nothing better, than
that a man should rejoice in his own works; for that is
his portion: for who shall bring him to see what shall be
after him?" This is what we must do. How can we? *It is
the gift of God.* When we come to the conclusion of the
argument and do not feel like rejoicing, this simply
means that we have been left behind in our folly, unable
to keep up the pace. Remember that all the objections
rehearsed in this section simply remain at the place
which Solomon had deliberately abandoned.

And the nature of these very old questions and
objections show how there really is nothing new under
the sun.

### Teach me thy statutes.

[16]And moreover I saw under the sun the place of
judgment, that wickedness was there; and the place of
righteousness, that iniquity was there. [17]I said in mine
heart, God shall judge the righteous and the wicked: for
there is a time there for every purpose and for every
work. (Eccl. 3:16–17)

So the first objection steps forward. "But . . . we see
wickedness in the courts." How can we say that God sits
on the throne of High Justice when our judges, who are
appointed on earth to reflect that justice, do not care to
do so (3:16)? How can He be up there when *they* are
down *here?* Problems in the judiciary did not begin with
our liberal justices in this century; Solomon knew of
many who twisted words behind the bench. Now the
wickedness of our judges provides material for this
common slander against the truth. However, Solomon

hastens to add that God will put it all to rights in the final judgment (3:17).

When men depart from the Word of God and are entrusted with power, they come to believe that they *are* the law. The robe completes the illusion, both for us and for them. For some time after the transition, we all still chant mantras like *the rule of law, not of men,* but no one understands it anymore. No way can be found to bring men under a law independent of the whims and wishes of capricious men, apart from a formal recognition of that hard master of biblical law.

Evangelical Christians, who ought to know better, have contented themselves for some years now in voting for the lesser of two evils. One faction wants to drive toward the cliff of God's judgment at sixty miles an hour, while the loyal opposition wants to slow down to forty. Hard-working and soft-thinking Christians bust a gut to get the latter group into power. And then, when they do assume control, they compromise with the ousted group and settle on a moderate and well-respected speed of fifty-eight.[†]

But the Bible prohibits establishing a ruler— whether a ruler or judge—who does not fear God. "Moreover thou shalt provide out of all the people able men, such as fear God, men of truth, hating covetousness; and place such over them, to be rulers of thousands, and rulers of hundreds, rulers of fifties, and rulers of tens" (Ex. 18:21). Instead of this, we appoint fools and imbeciles, men who do not fear God, men who love deceit, kickbacks, and bribes, and then we wonder why our traditional values campaign always seems to bog down. "Why, O Lord, dost thou not deliver us from the secularists?" Of course, the answer is that we haven't stopped voting for them. We are like those who want to be delivered from drowning so long as they get to stay down at the bottom of the pool.

But the check that God provides against tyranny in the courts is a knowledge of the coming judgment. It is not surprising that those rulers and judges who do not believe in this judgment are not restrained by it. But the *odd* thing is that countless thousands who do believe in this judgment believe it to be irrelevant in political considerations. Only a fool entrusts a man with real power over his fellows when that man does not fear God. "I said in mine heart, God shall judge the righteous and the wicked" (v. 17).

This verse promising judgment is *very important* as we come to the next section, because many have assumed that Solomon has a perspective that is entirely centered on this world and its events. As this passage shows, the last judgment is very much in view throughout this book of wisdom. And of course we must also remember the last verse of the book. So the answer to the objection founded on the existence of judicial oppression is that the gift of God bestows knowledge of the final judgment. This knowledge of ultimate justice puts every judicial monstrosity in perspective. In a day when judicial monstrosities grow like thistles in sunshine, we need the encouragement.

**Make me to understand the way of thy precepts.**
[18]I said in mine heart concerning the estate of the sons of men, that God might manifest them, and that they might see that they themselves are beasts. [19]For that which befalleth the sons of men befalleth beasts; even one thing befalleth them: as the one dieth, so dieth the other; yea,

they have all one breath; so that a man hath no preeminence above a beast: for all is vanity. ²⁰All go unto one place; all are of the dust, and all turn to dust again. ²¹Who knoweth the spirit of man that goeth upward, and the spirit of the beast that goeth downward to the earth? ²²Wherefore I perceive that there is nothing better, than that a man should rejoice in his own works; for that is his portion: for who shall bring him to see what shall be after him? (Eccl. 3:18–22)

Another objection volunteers. "But . . . men and animals both die." This is the mortality test (3:18). God makes sure that we can see with our own eyes that we go down into the ground just like the dogs and pigs. So on what basis do we say there is a difference between us? The only possible basis is a transcendent statement from outside the system, a statement given by God's Word. When we look at verse 21, remember verse 17. Solomon has just finished teaching us about a final judgment. But given the parameters of autonomy, what difference is there? This is not a relativistic question. Solomon does not ask: *who knows? who can say?* This should be understood as having an implied indicative statement contained within it. The spirit of man does go up; the spirit of an animal does go down. But who knows this? God does, but man on his own *cannot*.

Men know they are in a separate category from the animals. Solomon's point is that they cannot consistently know this, given their epistemology. Look what happens to the carcasses of each. The *imago Dei* does not retard the process of corruption. Consequently, if that is where we look in order to discover that image, then we will come to nothing but despair. In the last analysis,

scientism can only measure how fast we rot. Knowledge
of the final judgment and how men as men will stand
there before a great throne does not come from dissect-
ing frogs.

Some fevered greens have sought to swallow the
*reductio.* "Fine," they say, "man is no different from the
animals. Every life is on the same level." And then they
go on to urge us to save the whales, like we were in
charge of them or something. The uniqueness of man
can be denied, but cannot be made to disappear. Men will
always be men, but apart from an acknowledgment of the
final judgment, they cannot hope to give a reasonable
account of themselves as men.

So we must remember to look ahead to 12:7. The
answer to this mortality objection is that the gift of God
*bestows knowledge of our life after death.*

### Strengthen thou me according unto thy word.
[1]So I returned, and considered all the oppressions that
are done under the sun: and behold the tears of such as
were oppressed, and they had no comforter; and on the
side of their oppressors there was power; but they had no
comforter. [2]Wherefore I praised the dead which are
already dead more than the living which are yet alive.
[3]Yea, better is he than both they, which hath not yet
been, who hath not seen the evil work that is done under
the sun. (Eccl. 4:1–3)

But the objections do not cease. "But . . . men are
oppressed." Men are not only oppressed by the courts
specifically, as discussed earlier. They are oppressed
generally throughout their lives in business, in marriage,
in various relationships, by anyone with power (4:1). It

is better to be dead or unborn than oppressed this way
(4:2–3).

Men who are already dead are better off than the
men still alive, or the men not yet born. In this life,
oppressors have power, and they use it. The one oppressed may cry and still find that he has no comforter.

We are born to trouble as the sparks fly upward.
Nothing can be accomplished by denying the existence of
this trouble; the only thing we are to do is look forward
to death when we will be out of the oppressors's reach.
Solomon has already reminded us of the judgment, and
he will remind us of it again. If we understand this, if we
remember, then we will leave this wilderness and come to
comfort.

So the answer here is that the gift of God *bestows
comfort*.


### Grant me thy law graciously.

⁴Again, I considered all travail, and every right work, that
for this a man is envied of his neighbour. This is also
vanity and vexation of spirit. ⁵The fool foldeth his hands
together, and eateth his own flesh. ⁶Better is an handful
with quietness, than both the hands full with travail and
vexation of spirit. (Eccl. 4:4–6)

So another objection comes. "But . . . men are
envious and lazy." This really is the flip side of the
previous problem: before, we saw the powerful kicking
the powerless, but now we see the powerless spitting at
those who have exercised a creative dominion. When a
man works hard and accomplishes much, his neighbor
envies him (4:4–6). The man who envies is often a
cannibal, devouring himself (v. 5). But hard work alone

can also be unsatisfying (v. 6).

When a man works hard—and does well—his neighbor carps at him. "It is all very well for *you* to talk—you have it easy!" Of course he has it easy, because he has worked hard and is now enjoying the fruit of his labor. His neighbor sees it as unfair and vexes himself over the problem considerably.

Unscrupulous demagogues then arise and promise to make the rich pay their "fair share." This is a complex and long-standing ritual in which the poor are fleeced in the name of fleecing the rich. The poor allow it to happen because they are blinded by their envy. Any man seeking control of the engines of the state, the better to accomplish his plundering, always promises to make the great businesses pay taxes—and the envious man cheers. But of course, no business ever paid a tax without passing it on to the consumer, and so the envious man finds himself paying for the pillage he ardently supports. But don't feel sorry for him; he is an envious fool and deserves everything he gets, both good and hard.

A wise man hates all forms of envy. The answer given by Solomon is that the gift of God *bestows satisfaction in your own toil.*

### I have chosen the way of truth.

[7]Then I returned, and I saw vanity under the sun. [8]There is one alone, and there is not a second; yea, he hath neither child nor brother: yet is there no end of all his labour; neither is his eye satisfied with riches; neither saith he, For whom do I labour, and bereave my soul of good? This is also vanity, yea, it is a sore travail. [9]Two are better than one; because they have a good reward for their labour. [10]For if they fall, the one will lift up his

fellow: but woe to him that is alone when he falleth; for he hath not another to help him up. ¹¹Again, if two lie together, then they have heat: but how can one be warm alone? ¹²And if one prevail against him, two shall withstand him; and a threefold cord is not quickly broken. (Eccl. 4:7–12)

Still another argument. "But . . . men are lonely." A hard-working miser is lonely and industrious, but has no reason for what he does (4:7–8). Man is built for community, and loneliness is a great evil. Working together is satisfying; it is fruitful, prevents harm, keeps you warm, defends, and keeps unity (4:9–12).

A man works hard to make a pile and doesn't stop to ask a very basic question—why am I doing this? He makes a stack of money but has no one to share it with. He can't afford to marry or have children, because they would take him away from his work. He cannot afford to have friends because all their motives would be suspect. He could buy dinner for everyone in the restaurant, but no one wants to sit with him. That's all right, because he doesn't want to sit with them either.

But companionship is dear. God created us for friendship, and a curse resides on all things which prevent men from forming friendships. One of the great culprits in this affair is the task of making big-time money.

So the answer is that the gift of God *bestows companionship.*

### Thy judgments have I laid before me.

¹³Better is a poor and a wise child than an old and foolish king, who will no more be admonished. ¹⁴For out

of prison he cometh to reign; whereas also he that is born in his kingdom becometh poor. [15]I considered all the living which walk under the sun, with the second child that shall stand up in his stead. [16]There is no end of all the people, even of all that have been before them: they also that come after shall not rejoice in him. Surely this also is vanity and vexation of spirit.
(Eccl. 4:13–16)

So the last objection is mustered. "But . . . fame is transient." This is the scriptural original of Warhol's famous dictum that everyone will get their fifteen minutes of fame (v. 4). An old king grew inflexible and unwilling to listen. He was replaced by a youth who was followed by hordes . . . but he in his turn will become unpopular.

This is the way it goes, and that is well. This is how God established it. When we refuse to be swept along with every new political excitement, when we learn that this has all happened many times before, we will have grown a measure in wisdom. As Augustine put it, in our great affairs, the dead are always replaced by the dying. The currently unpopular are always replaced by those who are not yet unpopular. But they will be, and so the wise must seek a better vantage. The answer here is that the gift of God *bestows acceptance with Him.*

We should welcome the silence of despair. Human despair has no authority to contradict what God gives to us. It may only contradict what *it* experiences, *i.e.,* life under the sun. Without God and without His Word, what can we say about such things? We have to be silent. We must despair . . . of our despair.

## Overview and Review

First division (1:2–2:26): We should know by now that satisfaction cannot come from anything within man's power.

Second division (3:1–5:20): Because God is sovereign over every last little thing, Solomon must answer objections to the doctrine. First subdivision (3:1–3:15): God in His sovereignty places everything in its place with perfection of judgment. Second subdivision (3:16–4:16): Six objections to God's sovereignty are addressed.

Third division (6:1–8:15): Having established it, Solomon applies his doctrine that the sovereign God alone gives the power to enjoy vanity.

Fourth division (8:16–12:14): The last section of the book is a miscellany, removing various obstacles and addressing practical concerns.

# A Sacrifice of Fools

*But let your communication be, Yea, yea; Nay, nay: for whatsoever is more than these cometh of evil.*

Matthew 5:37

We have seen that the theme of Ecclesiastes is that enjoyment and pleasure are by grace through faith, and not of works, lest any man should boast. The admonitions we find in this passage are not the way for us to *earn* enjoyment but rather the characteristics of such enjoyment. A fool approaches God in a fashion inconsistent with the truth, wisdom, or joy. The wise *listen* and listen up.

Theoretical objections to God's sovereignty have been addressed in the previous section. Solomon now turns to some practical obstacles which hinder an understanding of this truth. Obviously, at least two things can interfere with our understanding of the glorious truth of *who God is*. The first is how we think about God, and the second is how we *live* before God. So in this section Solomon now cautions us against offering up the practical worship of fools.

**I will run the way of thy commandments.**
¹Keep thy foot when thou goest to the house of God, and be more ready to hear, than to give the sacrifice of fools: for they consider not that they do evil. ²Be not rash with thy mouth, and let not thine heart be hasty to utter any thing before God: for God is in heaven, and thou upon earth: therefore let thy words be few. ³For a dream cometh through the multitude of business; and a fool's voice is known by the multitude of words. (Eccl. 5:1–3)

So let us turn to consider the fool at his worship. Religiosity loves to bloviate before the Lord. Religious man loves his wordy prayers. A natural assumption for the flesh in religion is that God is somehow impressed with a word count, and all this despite an express scriptural injunction here to the contrary (5:1–3).

Our Lord prayed all night sometimes. "And it came to pass in those days, that he went out into a mountain to pray, and continued all night in prayer to God" (Luke 6:12). We are told to "pray without ceasing" (1 Thess. 5:17), and to be devoted to prayer (Col. 4:2). However, our introductory scriptural lessons in prayer clearly emphasize *brevity*. Being a prayer warrior—what an awful phrase for a wonderful thing!—is not the same as chattering, glibness, garrulousness, *etc.* Believers need to learn to offer few words first. This requires *composing* the thoughts. The fact that fools are wordy in prayer is not a law altered just because the words *in Jesus' name, amen* are attached to their prayers.

When Jesus taught his disciples to pray, He gave them a very simple and brief prayer. We are wiser than all that, and so our words gush forth. But He knew the heart of man, and so He attached an express warning. "But when ye pray, use not vain repetitions, as the heathen do: *for they think that they shall be heard for their much speaking*" (Matt. 6:7). "Gee," we wonder, "what does *that* mean?"

**Teach me, O Lord, the way of thy statutes.**
[4]When thou vowest a vow unto God, defer not to pay it; for he hath no pleasure in fools: pay that which thou hast vowed. [5]Better is it that thou shouldest not vow, than that thou shouldest vow and not pay. [6]Suffer not thy mouth to cause thy flesh to sin; neither say thou before the angel, that it was an error: wherefore should God be angry at thy voice, and destroy the work of thine hands? [7]For in the multitude of dreams and many words there are also divers vanities: but fear thou God. (Eccl. 5:4–7)

Fools love thoughtless vows as well. Talking about what you *will* do is a good, low-cost way to enhance your reputation down at the church. Think of a similar tactic employed by the late Ananias and Sapphira. This section of Ecclesiastes addresses a financial pledge, and then when a temple messenger comes to get it, the story told by the one who vowed is all different now (vv. 4–7). Dreamers like to talk, and talkers like to dream. Pay what you have vowed, because God takes no pleasure in fools. You do not want to set God against you in your work. *Fear the Lord.*

It is a matter of no little astonishment that so few people are concerned with whether God is for or against the work they are trying to accomplish. The prayer of the wise seeks the favor of the Lord upon the work done.

"And let the beauty of the LORD our God be upon us: and establish thou the work of our hands upon us; yea, the work of our hands establish thou it" (Ps. 90:17).

The fool disregards this duty and ignores the ramifications of having pledged to God something which he did not fulfill. If God were resolved to destroy a man's business, would it be difficult for Him to do? If God decided that financial ruin was going to be visited upon another fool today, would that be something that a man's financial analyst could stop?

**Give me understanding, and I shall keep thy law.**
[8]If thou seest the oppression of the poor, and violent perverting of judgment and justice in a province, marvel not at the matter: for he that is higher than the highest regardeth; and there be higher than they.

[9]Moreover the profit of the earth is for all: the king himself is served by the field. (Eccl. 5:8–9)

Religious fools also exhibit naïvete. Theological liberals come almost immediately to mind. It takes a certain kind of mind to think that world peace can be ushered in if we all hold hands and think happy thoughts. Arms are for hugging, and visualizing world peace is thought by some to be having quite an impact. But look around; look at the newspapers. Men are oppressed all the time—the wise are not amazed or embittered when it happens (vv. 8–9). The problem goes all the way up. But also remember that the king is as dependent upon agriculture as anyone else.

So a wise man does not become resentful at the petty tyrannies he sees in the provinces. The same rules govern in Washington. Men stand for office because they want to get into a position that would enable them to begin stealing money with a backhoe. This is affected in our nation somewhat by our very fine two-party system, which means that we have fierce debates about what color the backhoe should be. Only God, supreme above all, is immune from such corruptions.

Some men gravitate to the seat of political power, only to be disillusioned with the shocking avarice found there. Many others make themselves right at home in the corruption. Wise men know this without becoming bitter.

### Incline my heart unto thy testimonies.

[10]He that loveth silver shall not be satisfied with silver; nor he that loveth abundance with increase: this is also vanity. [11]When goods increase, they are increased that eat them: and what good is there to the owners thereof, saving the beholding of them with their eyes? (Eccl. 5:10–11)

This relates to covetousness. Lust always demands more, and then still more (vv. 10–17). But as Solomon teaches us here . . . *you can't take it with you*. This well-worn cliché is ignored as often as it is spoken—and frequently by the same people. But those who love silver and abundance are sleeping with false lovers who cannot satisfy (v. 10). An increase in goods brings with it an increase of accountants, lawyers, staff, managers, and scads of consultants with that hungry look in their eyes (v. 11).

Men who build empires frequently find themselves holding a grizzly bear by the ears. The more they do, the less they are able to do. The more control they amass, the less control they have. The more power they acquire, the more powerless they feel. This is because the vanity of increase, the futility of silver and gold, has a life of its own. A man may work hard to acquire money, only to discover at the end of the day that the money actually acquired him.

Few men have wealth, and even fewer control it when they do.

### Quicken thou me in thy way.

[12]The sleep of a labouring man is sweet, whether he eat little or much: but the abundance of the rich will not suffer him to sleep. [13]There is a sore evil which I have seen under the sun, namely, riches kept for the owners thereof to their hurt. [14]But those riches perish by evil travail: and he begetteth a son, and there is nothing in his hand. [15]As he came forth of his mother's womb, naked shall he return to go as he came, and shall take nothing of his labour, which he may carry away in his hand. [16]And this also is a sore evil, that in all points as he came, so shall he go: and what profit hath he that hath laboured for the wind? [17]All his days also he eateth in darkness, and he hath much sorrow and wrath with his sickness. (Eccl. 5:12–17)

Ditch diggers, Solomon tells us, sleep better than the anxiety-ridden rich (v. 12). A rich man who is a fool is destroyed by his own blessings (v. 13). If that rich man has a child, he will be born naked—the same condition his father will be in when he is born into the *next* world (vv. 14–15). A man arrives without possessions and he leaves without possessions. In the interval, while he *does* have all his stuff, he cannot sleep because he worries about it. What a deal. But if he works hard and frets and worries a whole lot, he can make sure that his fine clothes (for the short time he *does* have them) are nothing but nice wrapping paper for ulcers (v. 17).

Solomon calls it a sore evil. Here he is, there he goes. He labored all that while for the whistling wind, working to amass his very own treasury of balloon juice. For that reward he ate his meals in darkness, suffered his sorrow and wrath, and added it all to his sickness. Better him than me.

The exhortation is plain. Fear God, and reject the idiocy of greed . . . that great choker of quiet wisdom.

Turn away mine eyes from beholding vanity. [18]Behold that which I have seen: it is good and comely for one to eat and to drink, and to enjoy the good of all his labour that he taketh under the sun all the days of his life, which God giveth him: for it is his portion. [19]Every man also to whom God hath given riches and wealth, and hath given him power to eat thereof, and to take his portion, and to rejoice in his labour; this is the gift of God. [20]For he shall not much remember the days of his life; because God answereth him in the joy of his heart. (Ecclesiastes 5:18–20)

The conclusion of this cynical line of argument is peace and joy. In verses 18–20, the crucial phrases are these: *and given him power to eat of it* and *this is the gift of God.* God, as part of the goodness of His grace, keeps a man occupied with his stuff, giving him joy. The fact that some men can just take it as it comes, without agonizing all the time over the ultimate meaning of things, *is the gift of God* (v. 20).

We need to turn back and look at the territory covered by Solomon's argument. According to carnal reason, this is truly an odd conclusion. Solomon is telling us what he has *seen*, and this includes what he has been describing in the verses leading up to this conclusion. But it also includes what he sees in this conclusion. It is good and comely to lift the cup and eat good bread. A man can receive his portion of labor under the sun, and he may receive it gladly. When a man receives what God gives—and only then—he may thoroughly enjoy himself. His portion is sweet when it is received as a gift. But if it is just there, unexamined, taken for granted, mountains of it will only add to the despair.

When God gives power for enjoyment, a man may thrive, even though he lives his days under a dying sun.

### Overview and Review

First division (1:2–2:26): We, along with the Stones, can't get no satisfaction. Nothing from within man's power can enable him to *taste*.

Second division (3:1–5:20): The book of Ecclesiastes is an explicitly Calvinistic book. God is sovereign over everything, but objections must be answered. First subdivision (3:1–3:15): God in His sovereignty arranges everything according to his good counsel. Second subdivision (3:16–4:16): Six objections to God's sovereignty are raised and answered. Third subdivision (5:1–5:20): Given the sovereignty of God, practical applications and cautions have to be covered.

Third division (6:1–8:15): Solomon applies his doctrine that God alone gives power to taste the vanity.

Fourth division (8:16–12:14): The last section removes various obstacles and discouragements.

# A Right Judgment

*It is easier for a camel to go through the eye of a needle, than for a rich man to enter into the kingdom of God.*

Matthew 19:24

We see many apparent inequalities and injustices in the way God governs the world. We conclude (although some do not say so out loud) that God is unjust. A major part of our problem is that we weigh the evidence with the wrong scales. We think, for example, that an injustice has been done because one man is wealthy and another poor. But there is more to the story.

### Let thy judgments help me.

[1]There is an evil which I have seen under the sun, and it is common among men: [2]A man to whom God hath given riches, wealth, and honour, so that he wanteth nothing for his soul of all that he desireth, yet God giveth him not power to eat thereof, but a stranger eateth it: this is vanity, and it is an evil disease. [3]If a man beget an hundred children, and live many years, so that the days of his years be many, and his soul be not filled with good, and also that he have no burial; I say, that an untimely birth

is better than he. ⁴For he cometh in with vanity, and departeth in darkness, and his name shall be covered with darkness. ⁵Moreover he hath not seen the sun, nor known any thing: this hath more rest than the other. ⁶Yea, though he live a thousand years twice told, yet hath he seen no good: do not all go to one place? ⁷All the labour of man is for his mouth, and yet the appetite is not filled. ⁸For what hath the wise more than the fool? what hath the poor, that knoweth to walk before the living? ⁹Better is the sight of the eyes than the wandering of the desire: this is also vanity and vexation of spirit. ¹⁰That which hath been is named already, and it is known that it is man: neither may he contend with him that is mightier than he. ¹¹Seeing there be many things that increase vanity, what is man the better? ¹²For who knoweth what is good for man in this life, all the days of his vain life which he spendeth as a shadow? for who can tell a man what shall be after him under the sun? (Eccl. 6:1–12)

The limits of prosperity are set by God. Prosperity is not necessarily good (Eccl. 6:1–12). We want to evaluate everything that parades by us *simply*, and say that material blessings are always a blessing and that adversity is always a curse. It is not necessarily so. We cannot necessarily tell God's disposition toward a man through his *outward* condition.

We are all familiar with the man who has everything. God frequently gives men many external blessings—without giving them the spiritual taste buds to enjoy what they have. This is a sore affliction from the Lord. If we understand the point here, we metaphorically see a man without any taste buds who can afford the finest of

restaurants. The finest chef in the world can only fix him
gray, cold oatmeal. We may see an impotent man married
to a beautiful woman. The wise would do well to guard
their hearts and to refuse to envy a bed where nothing
happens. The people most often envied are frequently
the most miserable people on the face of the earth. It
would have been better for them to have never been born
(vv. 1–6).

The law of reciprocity is obvious. We work to eat
and eat to work. We labor away in a tight, little circle.
Our mouths and stomachs demand it of us. It is better
to enjoy what you have than to have a "wandering desire." But apart from the grace of God, *we cannot* enjoy
working in order to eat (vv. 7–9).

We all are under the hand of God. Men cannot
break out of this condition. What a man is has been
"named already." A man's arms are too short to box with
God. Apart from the gift of God, the more a man
struggles with his condition, the more the vanity in-
creases (vv. 10–12).

If God does not give the power of enjoyment, then a
man cannot help himself. Like Tantalus in Hades,
everything he reaches for retreats from him. It is a cold
fact that God does in fact give many goods to men who
are not given the corresponding power to eat those
goods. The good Lord gives to His people a can opener
to go with the cans of peaches He gives them. But to the
unbeliever, He gives no way of genuine enjoyment. This
being the case, it does not matter how many cans a man
might accumulate. Do we measure satisfaction by what
we may stack up, or by what we are given to enjoy? What
is the wealthy unbeliever going to do? Lick the picture
there on the label?

The fool cannot enjoy the goodness of the earth. The wise man can do so, but not because of any wisdom inherent in him. He is the recipient of a gift.

## Thy judgments are good.

¹A good name is better than precious ointment; and the day of death than the day of one's birth. ²It is better to go to the house of mourning, than to go to the house of feasting: for that is the end of all men; and the living will lay it to his heart. ³Sorrow is better than laughter: for by the sadness of the countenance the heart is made better. ⁴The heart of the wise is in the house of mourning; but the heart of fools is in the house of mirth. ⁵It is better to hear the rebuke of the wise, than for a man to hear the song of fools. ⁶For as the crackling of thorns under a pot, so is the laughter of the fool: this also is vanity.

⁷Surely oppression maketh a wise man mad; and a gift destroyeth the heart. ⁸Better is the end of a thing than the beginning thereof: and the patient in spirit is better than the proud in spirit. ⁹Be not hasty in thy spirit to be angry: for anger resteth in the bosom of fools. ¹⁰Say not thou, What is the cause that the former days were better than these? for thou dost not inquire wisely concerning this.

¹¹Wisdom is good with an inheritance: and by it there is profit to them that see the sun. ¹²For wisdom is a defence, and money is a defence: but the excellency of knowledge is, that wisdom giveth life to them that have it. (Eccl. 7:1–12)

In these proverbs we find a contrast made to the earlier point. Just as prosperity is not necessarily a blessing, so adversity is not necessarily a bad thing

(Eccl. 7:1–12). We are familiar with the picture of a
spoiled rich child with a family room full of expensive
toys. He sits there in the corner, engaged in a furious
sulk. Meantime, across town another little boy is filled
with the goodness of life, running around in his back
yard all afternoon, wonderfully occupied with a stick. Is
the room full of toys a blessing? Only on the surface. Is
the poverty of the stick an adversity? Not at all—it is a
gnarled key that opens the doors of many worlds. Many
of us remember with great fondness how blessed we were
with such *rich* toys.

A good man wants a good name. Precious ointment
is a great blessing, but a good name is better (v. 1). If a
man had to choose between the two, the choice would be
a simple one . . . if the man were a wise one.

The day of death is approaching each of us. The day
of birth appears to have great promise. But the day of
death is better (v. 1). Is a man suffering adversity
because he comes to death? If he has lived in wisdom, his
inevitable death is gain. To live is Christ, to die is *gain*.
But the day of death is only better for those who know
that it is and why it is.

Both mourning and feasting are from the Lord. But
mourning is better than *empty* mirth. The vapid world of
sitcoms and stand-up chortlings is a bunch of nothing
(vv. 2–4). A man who knows how to mourn will also
know the meaning of solid laughter. But if a man does
not know the wisdom of mourning, then no amount of
tittering will fill up his soul.

Admonition and rebuke bring another kind of
adversity. But it is far better to hear them than to listen
to the party songs of fools (vv. 5–6). Pop radio did not
exist in Solomon's day, but it is not difficult to surmise

what he would have thought of it. If given a choice between hearing a wise man enumerate your faults and hearing the Spice Girls trying to sing something, the choice is an easy one.

A wise man can lose his reason under oppression or be debased with a bribe (v. 7). We might wish we could live in a world where wisdom was made out of stainless steel and could never degenerate . . . but we do not.

Wisdom is required to see ends and beginnings. The proud in spirit boast at the beginning. The patient see it through to the end (v. 8). Here the ungodly Ahab had a measure of wisdom. A man who puts on his armor should not boast like the man who takes it off. The adversity of seeing something through is far better than the pleasure of bragging about something before it is done.

Fools do not understand patience or frustration. The righteous are not those who never get angry. But the righteous certainly are *slow* to anger. Men who are quick to anger have posted their mailbox by the road, a box which says "a fool lives here" (v. 9). A quick-tempered man is simply a walking display case of folly. "A fool's wrath is presently known: but a prudent man covereth shame" (Prov. 12:16). We are called to be quick to listen, slow to speak, and *slow* to become angry. Our Lord was angry in the incident of the man's withered hand, but the end result of His anger was a healing and glory given to God. The end result of man's anger is broken crockery.

We must also understand ongoing affliction. Why should we moan about the "bad turn" events have taken? Why are we no longer in the "good old days?" The answer is that God does not want us to be. *He* is the Governor of all. Further affliction may be necessary (vv. 10–12).

Sometimes the good old days were not really that good. And even when they were, we must not revolt against God's wisdom in His providence. He is the one who decreed that those days would come to an end.

### Behold, I have longed after thy precepts.

[13]Consider the work of God: for who can make that straight, which he hath made crooked? [14]In the day of prosperity be joyful, but in the day of adversity consider: God also hath set the one over against the other, to the end that man should find nothing after him. [15]All things have I seen in the days of my vanity: there is a just man that perisheth in his righteousness, and there is a wicked man that prolongeth his life in his wickedness. (Eccl. 7:13–15)

Follow the insight of wisdom. Consider the work of God in all these things. A wise man will never *kick against the goads*. Who can straighten what He has made crooked? Will a man be able to bend the world in a different direction than the Almighty has? This central doctrine in the book must be allowed to sink deeply into our souls. Is it crooked? Then the Lord God made it so. But why? If He had wanted us to know that, then He would have told us. The closest we get to an explanation is found in Romans 9—

> What if God, willing to shew his wrath, and to
> make his power known, endured with much
> longsuffering the vessels of wrath fitted to

destruction: And that he might make known the
riches of his glory on the vessels of mercy, which
he had afore prepared unto glory, even us, whom
he hath called, not of the Jews only, but also of
the Gentiles?

(Rom. 9:22–24)

The ultimate explanation is that God does all things to
glorify His name and exalt His majesty. But regardless of
various reasons for the crookedness of the world, the fact
remains that the Bible affirms God's sovereignty over the
crooked. He truly is the only Lord.

We are to receive our prosperity *as* from Him
because it *is* from Him (v. 14). But in the day of adversity, we are also to remember our doctrine on the sovereignty of God. He has made *both* days (v. 14). The Lord
brings the springtime, and the Lord brings earthquakes.
The Lord gives the birthday, and the Lord assigns the
day of mourning. Job counseled his wife correctly. She
was talking as though she had adopted the theology of
the foolish women. "But he said unto her, Thou speakest
as one of the foolish women speaketh. What? shall we
receive good at the hand of God, and shall we not receive
evil? In all this did not Job sin with his lips" (Job 2:10).
The church today is dominated by this theology of silly
women. God never does *bad* things; He only does good
things. He makes pussy willows and kittens, not thunder,
lightning, and blue rain.

We worship God, who is Inscrutable Wisdom. What
we see with our eyes does not settle the matter.

**Overview and Review**

First division (1:2–2:26): Satisfaction does not come from within man.

Second division (3:1–5:20): God is sovereign over everything. Objections are set aside.

Third division (6:1–8:15): Solomon applies his doctrine that the sovereign God alone gives enjoyment in vanity. First subdivision (6:1–7:15): We must evaluate our outward condition properly.

Fourth division (8:16–12:14): The last section clears up remaining problems.

# Tiny Little Souls and Tight Little Shoes

*But when his disciples saw it, they had indignation, saying, To what purpose is this waste? For this ointment might have been sold for much, and given to the poor.*

Matthew 26:8–9

In the previous section we saw that all is not as it appears to us. Prosperity may be a camouflaged curse; a man may be surrounded with untasted wealth. Adversity may be the means by which God is bringing great blessing; as Rutherford knew, when in the cellar of affliction, a man can find God's choicest wines. All situations are not what they appear.

In this section, we see that all *men* are not as they appear. We may be drawing wrong conclusions about the world around us because we judge based on external experiences. But Christ forbade all surface judgments.

### I have hoped in thy judgments.

[16]Be not righteous over much; neither make thyself over wise: why shouldest thou destroy thyself? [17]Be not over much wicked, neither be thou foolish: why shouldest thou die before thy time? [18]It is good that thou

shouldest take hold of this; yea, also from this withdraw not thine hand: for he that feareth God shall come forth of them all. ¹⁹Wisdom strengtheneth the wise more than ten mighty men which are in the city. ²⁰For there is not a just man upon earth, that doeth good, and sinneth not. ²¹Also take no heed unto all words that are spoken; lest thou hear thy servant curse thee: ²²For oftentimes also thine own heart knoweth that thou thyself likewise hast cursed others. (Eccl. 7:16–22)

What does it mean to be overly righteous? Of course God is perfectly righteous; this does not mean He has taken it to an extreme. Clearly Solomon here is not addressing genuine piety, righteousness, or wisdom. He is speaking of what all too often *passes for it*. So what does this mean? Not to put too fine a point on it, it means . . . Nice Christian. Priggish Christian. Sanctimonious Christian. Tight-shoes Christian. Pursed lips Christian. Stickler Christian. Insufferable Christian. Prudish Christian. Doctrinally correct Christian. Know-it-all Christian. Ostentatious Christian. Quiet-time-every-day-or-I'll-go-to-Hell Christian. Conceited Christian. Orthodox Christian. *UnChristian* Christian.

The fact that Christ did a marvelous demolition job on the reputation of the Pharisees often obscures for us the fact that, before His assaults, they generally had a good reputation among the people for their piety. They were a well-respected group of conservative theologians. What men like in religion is not necessarily what God likes. What men admire is not necessarily what God admires. "And he said unto them, Ye are they which justify yourselves before men; but God knoweth your hearts: for that which is highly esteemed among men is abomination in the sight of God" (Luke 16:15).

We are not to be autonomous, whether it is autonomously good or autonomously bad. We are not to be self-willed in evil. It is suicide. But neither are we to be self-willed in doing what *we* define as good. It is self-destruction (vv. 16–17). We all know about those characters who shake their fists at heaven and how there is then a sharp intake of breath all around the sanctuary. But then we, in the grip of what we feel must be right and true, do precisely the opposite of what the Bible says to do. The examples of this religiosity were plentiful in Christ's day, and their tribe does not appear to have diminished in the intervening time. We say that the body is the temple of the Holy Spirit and so we must abstain from tobacco. Paul said that he was talking about sexual immorality and went on to add that he was not talking about any other sin whatever. But we still *feel* like smoking must be ungodly, and so we stick to our guns. Christ said not to pray in order to be seen by men; we organize prayer meetings on the Capitol steps in the hope that CBS will cover it. We say that alcohol must be sin because some frantic women in the nineteenth century decided it was. The Lord made about one hundred and sixty gallons of the best wine in order to help the festivities along. And wisdom is vindicated by her children.

The antidote to this religiosity is the fear of God and *not* a pagan moderation. If a man fears God sincerely, then he will not fall into religious foolishness (v. 18). True wisdom is strength, while the desire to *appear* wise is suicide. True wisdom, as the skateboarding youth of today might say, rocks the house (v. 19). Not that they know anything about it.

The religious bustle of those who do not know God

can be considerable. The lies, pretenses, and hypocrisies can be polished up to shine like marble. And one of the great pretenses in all the activity is the notion that the people involved in all the holy hubbub do not sin. But everyone sins. Judge men according to Scripture, Solomon says, and not by appearances down at the church (v. 20). *Everyone sins.*

This is why Solomon warns us not to be hyper over the sins of others. Suppose a man hears someone curse him? Not to worry—cut him a little bit of slack. Maybe the one who overhears has done that kind of thing himself a time or two. He shouldn't run around applying the disciplinary procedures of Matthew 18 to everything that moves (vv. 21–22). There is a zeal for righteousness which does not know its own spirit (Luke 9:55).

The upshot is that not everything "righteous" is all that good. Not everything "sinful" is all that bad. Only a fool jumps to pious and edifying conclusions.

### Let thy mercies come also unto me.

[23]All this have I proved by wisdom: I said, I will be wise; but it was far from me. [24]That which is far off, and exceeding deep, who can find it out? [25]I applied mine heart to know, and to search, and to seek out wisdom, and the reason of things, and to know the wickedness of folly, even of foolishness and madness: [26]And I find more bitter than death the woman, whose heart is snares and nets, and her hands as bands: whoso pleaseth God shall escape from her; but the sinner shall be taken by her. [27]Behold, this have I found, saith the preacher, counting one by one, to find out the account: [28]Which yet my soul seeketh, but I find not: one man among a thousand have

I found; but a woman among all those have I not found.
(Eccl. 7:23–28)

While ultimate wisdom comes from beyond the sun,
Solomon had seen much by wisdom under the sun
(v. 23). He proved and tested it by wisdom. At the same
time, when he said, "I will be wise," it immediately fled
from him (v. 23–24). Despite the limitations, some
things—like the wickedness of folly—he *can* know. He
turns to consider sexual folly.

There is a woman who hunts by night, whose trap is
pleasantly baited. Like a hunter who understands the
prey, an immoral woman knows how to get the results
she wants (v. 26a). "For a whore is a deep ditch; and a
strange woman is a narrow pit. She also lieth in wait as
for a prey, and increaseth the transgressors among men"
(Prov. 23:27–28). Not that the task is all that hard . . .
no more than trying to hit the ground with your hat.
Only the pleasure of God can rescue a man from her.
Immoral men tell themselves they are escaping God's
restrictions at the very moment when they are falling
into the trap which *He* has set for them (v. 26b). One
writer has commented that men in revolt against God
will either raise the fist in civil unrest and revolution or
raise the phallus in their contemptuous fornications.[†] In
that fornication they revolt against sexual maturity and
show their bestial ignorance of the *imago Dei*.

In this, men think they are escaping from God in
their fornications and adulteries. "The mouth of strange
women is a deep pit: he that is abhorred of the Lord
shall fall therein" (Prov. 22:14). But the only one who
escapes is the one who pleases God (v. 26). Foolish men
believe they have found sexual liberty at just the moment

when God has seized them by their yearning little idol in order to dash them against the rocks. Their exhilarating sensation of liberty is only temporary—a free fall with death at the end of it.

In this, Solomon can speak from his own experience. Looking for wisdom, he found one man in a thousand, and no women (v. 28). Now Solomon elsewhere extols feminine wisdom (indeed he *personifies* Wisdom as a woman in Proverbs 8). But in his own search, Solomon had found virtually no men of integrity at his court, and in the rest of his study, conducted largely with the lights down low, he found no women of integrity in his harem. This observation is no grounds for a masculinist pride. Even with this limited range of people, the men are only one tenth of one percent better than the women. The point is clear: men of integrity at Solomon's court were extremely rare, and women of integrity were non-existent.

### Take not the word of truth utterly out of my mouth.

[29]Lo, this only have I found, that God hath made man upright; but they have sought out many inventions. (Eccl. 7:29)

The heart of man has fashioned many devices. In our creation, we were made upright in Adam. He rebelled, and since that time we have been using the gifts given us by God to destroy ourselves. Some of them are obvious, like the rope of wickedness and rebellion. We use our defiance as the means to hang ourselves, as Judas did, from a high tree.

The other kind of device is the trick of the self-righteous. This is a slow-acting poison which corrupts and pollutes the inner man. The religiously self-righteous are, to use the great words of Calhoun, like a dead mackerel on the beach in the moonlight. They "simultaneously shine and stink." What religious men esteem is not what God esteems. Our prayers need to be prayed for. Our tears need washing. Our repentance needs to be repented of.

God made us upright; we have sought out many schemes. The righteousness of Another is the *only* answer.

### Overview and Review

First division (1:2–2:26): Satisfaction cometh not from man.

Second division (3:1–5:20): For those just joining us, God is sovereign over everything, which is to say, God is God. Solomon answers the perennial objections to this unobjectionable doctrine.

Third division (6:1–8:15): Only God gives the power to enjoy vanity. First subdivision (6:1–7:15): We must evaluate our outward condition properly. Second subdivision (7:16–29): We must evaluate men properly.

Fourth division (8:16–12:14): The last section deals with various details and remaining concerns.

# Walking in the Corridors of Power

*The same day there came certain of the Pharisees, saying unto him,*
*Get thee out, and depart hence: for Herod will kill thee. And he said*
*unto them, Go ye, and tell that fox, Behold, I cast out devils, and I*
*do cures today and tomorrow, and the third day I shall be perfected.*
Luke 13:31–32

As we consider the apparent inequities of our lives under
the sun, this section of Ecclesiastes has taught us that we
must evaluate the situation properly—affliction is not
always bad and prosperity not always good. By the same
token, we have learned that we must evaluate men
properly. The righteous are not always all *that* righteous,
and the wicked are not always as bad as we might think
they are. Now we must come to see that righteous
government, even in a fallen world, could ameliorate
some of the apparent inequities. At the same time, we
know that the amelioration of evil is not the same thing
as the entire removal of evil . . . and anyway, this possible
lessening of evil does not always happen.

**I will speak of thy testimonies also before kings.** ¹Who is as the wise man? and who knoweth the interpretation of a thing? a man's wisdom maketh his face to shine, and the boldness of his face shall be changed. ²I counsel thee to keep the king's commandment, and that in regard of the oath of God. ³Be not hasty to go out of his sight: stand not in an evil thing; for he doeth whatsoever pleaseth him. ⁴Where the word of a king is, there is power: and who may say unto him, What doest thou? ⁵Whoso keepeth the commandment shall feel no evil thing: and a wise man's heart discerneth both time and judgment.

⁶Because to every purpose there is time and judgment, therefore the misery of man is great upon him. ⁷For he knoweth not that which shall be: for who can tell him when it shall be? ⁸There is no man that hath power over the spirit to retain the spirit; neither hath he power in the day of death: and there is no discharge in that war; neither shall wickedness deliver those that are given to it. (Eccl. 8:1–8)

The Word gives counsel to both king and courtier, and so we find instruction here for those who would influence the king. This does not assume an "across the board" approval of the king in power; in fact, it assumes the opposite. A wise man in the presence of the king can give the interpretation of a thing, and his wisdom makes his face to shine (v. 1). A number of instructions are given to a courtier in such a position—the courtier who would be wise at court.

The first thing to consider is an oath of allegiance.[1] Remember that no pledge of loyalty to a sinner can be absolute, but it can nevertheless be genuine and lawful.

The courtier is to be loyal because of his oath (v. 2). Treachery is the currency of power-mongers; the godly are to have no part of it.

A wise courtier must avoid falling on his sword, avoid an "all or nothing" mentality. He should not be hasty in departing from the court (full of zeal for his vetoed proposals). He must not engage in evil designs (v. 3). If relativists seek after hollow minds, the godly must not respond by building minds of solid wood. Flexibility and prudence must not be confused with compromise and fear.

Prudence restrains a man in the same way that an oath does. The king has power. Who is in a position to give him backchat? (v. 4). Prudence is not necessarily cowardice or compromise. So a courtier picks his battles cautiously, careful not to die on every hill. The courtier must hold his peace and obey the king's commands. He must discern the right time and place to move; this is wisdom. The immediacy of suffering does not change this (vv. 5–6).

The ungodly king Ahab had a righteous cabinet minister, whom some believers would dismiss as a craven compromiser. How could a godly man serve in the government of such a man? The reasoning may seem good to us, but the Bible goes contrary to our reasoning.

> And Ahab called Obadiah, which was the governor of his house. . . . Now *Obadiah feared the LORD greatly*: For it was so, when Jezebel cut off the prophets of the LORD, that Obadiah took an hundred prophets, and hid them by fifty in a cave, and fed them with bread and water."
>
> (1 Kings 18:3–4)

The courtier is a mist giving advice to a king who is a mist—no one knows absolutely what will happen in days to come (v. 7). Everyone, king and courtier alike, is in a war with death. No one can keep the spirit contained in the body; no one is able to obtain a discharge from that coming fight, and all will lose it (v. 8). All political battles must therefore be kept in perspective. No one is able to fight the final war between light and dark here under the sun, and no one should pretend to try.

**So shall I keep thy law continually for ever and ever.**

⁹All this have I seen, and applied my heart unto every work that is done under the sun: there is a time wherein one man ruleth over another to his own hurt. ¹⁰And so I saw the wicked buried, who had come and gone from the place of the holy, and they were forgotten in the city where they had so done: this is also vanity. ¹¹Because sentence against an evil work is not executed speedily, therefore the heart of the sons of men is fully set in them to do evil. ¹²Though a sinner do evil an hundred times, and his days be prolonged, yet surely I know that it shall be well with them that fear God, which fear before him: ¹³But it shall not be well with the wicked, neither shall he prolong his days, which are as a shadow; because he feareth not before God.

¹⁴There is a vanity which is done upon the earth; that there be just men, unto whom it happeneth according to the work of the wicked; again, there be wicked men, to whom it happeneth according to the work of the righteous: I said that this also is vanity. ¹⁵Then I commended mirth, because a man hath no better thing under the sun, than to eat, and to drink, and to be merry: for

that shall abide with him of his labour the days of his
life, which God giveth him under the sun.
(Eccl. 8:9–15)

Nevertheless, wickedness sometimes reigns. Men
sometimes rule over other men to their own hurt.
Imbecilic and evil policies do exist (v. 9). Wicked men
are sometimes buried with great honor and are granted
national holidays after a lifetime of trashing the place of
"holiness." This probably refers to the seat of judgment.
Justice should have been secure in this seat, but it was
not (v. 10). But then the wicked are in their own turn
forgotten. This also is vanity.

We know how it *could* work—swift justice does
provide a deterrent to crime (v. 11). Strike the fool and
the simple learn wisdom. Refuse to do so, and folly will
reign. Folly is wise enough to recognize a time of opportunity. Now we live in a time when the deterrent value of
swift justice is denied by the enlightened. But the godly
know what swarms of sociologists do not, and that is
that swift and sure punishment deters the wicked. This
obvious truth is stated here by Solomon.[2]

A man must remember the coming judgment.
Repeated success in sinning does not set aside the reality
of ultimate justice (vv. 12–13). While injustice can seem
to triumph—sometimes good men lose and wicked men
win (v. 14)—this apparent triumph is also vanity.

He who has ears to hear, let him hear it. To whom
this gift of God has been given, let him enjoy it. The
conclusion of the matter? What should a man do in a
world of powerful kings and wicked men who look as
though they got away with it? He should prepare to
make merry; he should enjoy himself—he should eat,

drink, and be merry all his days under the sun (v. 15). Again, Solomon comes to an unexpected conclusion. The fact that men wield power, sometimes unrighteously, is occasion to make merry and enjoy life with anyone else who has been given the gift of this wisdom.

## Overview and Review

First division (1:2–2:26): The power of enjoying anything does not arise from within man.

Second division (3:1–5:20): We know that God is sovereign over everything, but because some do not like knowing it, Solomon answers objections to the doctrine.

Third division (6:1–8:15): God alone gives the power to enjoy vanity. The teaching is applied. First subdivision (6:1–7:15): We must evaluate the outward condition of men properly. Second subdivision (7:16–29): We must also evaluate men properly. Third subdivision (8:1–15): The sin of powerful men can block the view.

Fourth division (8:16–12:14): Various obstacles and discouragements may remain in the minds of some, and so Solomon addresses these practical concerns.

# Loving Your Wife

*And the roof of thy mouth like the best wine for my beloved, that goeth down sweetly . . .*

Song of Songs 7:9

We should recall that Solomon is not just repeating himself throughout this book. His argument, cogent and compelling, *builds*. Throughout the course of his argument, he constantly returns to the basic lessons we must learn if we are to become wise, but he also constantly adds to this foundation.

**And 1 will delight myself in thy commandments.** [16]When I applied mine heart to know wisdom, and to see the business that is done upon the earth: (for also there is that neither day nor night seeth sleep with his eyes:) [17]Then I beheld all the work of God, that a man cannot find out the work that is done under the sun: because though a man labour to seek it out, yet he shall not find it; yea further; though a wise man think to know it, yet shall he not be able to find it. [1]For all this I considered in my heart even to declare all this, that the righteous, and the wise, and their works, are in the hand of God: no man knoweth either love or hatred by all that is before them. ²All things come alike to all: there is one event to the righteous, and to the wicked; to the good and to the clean, and to the unclean; to him that sacrificeth, and to him that sacrificeth not: as is the good, so is the sinner; and he that sweareth, as he that feareth an oath. ³This is an evil among all things that are done under the sun, that there is one event unto all: yea, also the heart of the sons of men is full of evil, and madness is in their heart while they live, and after that they go to the dead. (Eccl. 8:16–9:3)

Regardless of what we think, God is the Lord. We return now to a truth established earlier in the book. Again, wisdom of the sort urged by Solomon is not possible apart from a clear recognition of God's sovereignty over all things. Because he had a heart set to know, Solomon applied himself to this task. He set himself to know the business that was done *on the earth*. This was a task he set for himself, resulting in sleepless nights (v. 16).

But a man cannot know. The result was that he saw "all the work of God," and he also saw that a man *cannot know* what God is doing (v. 17). This is wisdom, wisdom discovered by a very wise man. The wise know how to identify what cannot be known. Solomon is not referring to the actions of God on the other side of the universe (which, of course, no one thinks we could know), but rather His governance of *our* lives *here* and *now*. He sets the limitation upon any man (v. 17) and not just upon himself and his own endeavors. Look around as you please, you do not know what is happening.

Wisdom does not seek to explain this sovereignty of

God. It is ironic that those who accept this truth are commonly accused of trying to explain the mechanics of God's sovereignty over "whatsoever comes to pass." But our ability to do this is something we emphatically deny. In this place, Solomon bluntly asserts *that* God controls all things. He does not say *how* God does it. Only a blockhead of the first order of magnitude would think to explain the way in which God reveals Himself through His works.

As we consider what passes before us, we cannot make sense of it. We tend to assume, echoing Shakespeare, that the history of all things is a tale told by an idiot, full of sound and fury, signifying nothing. But rather, it is a tale told *to* idiots. Both the righteous and the wicked *are in the hand of God*. We cannot tell what is occurring through what happens to them as far as we can see (9:1). Does God love me or hate me? The question cannot be answered through an appeal to external "blessings" or "curses." The real test is wisdom—a heart attitude of thankfulness and faith.

The man who curses and the man who blesses both get rained on (v. 1). A faithful man and an unfaithful man both get sunshine (vv. 2–3a). This is an "evil," but it is an evil which fits with the essential goodness of God. Confronted with the reality of it, we are to honor God as God and give Him thanks.

### ᗰᎽ hands also will I lift up unto thy commandments.

[4]For to him that is joined to all the living there is hope: for a living dog is better than a dead lion. [5]For the living know that they shall die: but the dead know not any thing, neither have they any more a reward; for the

memory of them is forgotten. ⁶Also their love, and their
hatred, and their envy, is now perished; neither have they
any more a portion for ever in any thing that is done
under the sun. (Eccl. 9:4–6)

Nevertheless, sin is madness. Notice how Solomon
slaps down human wisdom and autonomy. While *we*
cannot see any difference between the righteous and
wicked, yet it is *madness* to limit ourselves to our own
perspective. It is madness to not acknowledge God. And
yet men live this way while knowing that each of them
will die! Madness lives without faith, without eyes.

Today, while a man hears His voice, he must not
harden his heart. When a wicked man dies, his hope
perishes. It is appointed to man to die once and after
that the judgment. In this context, Solomon says that to
be alive as a contemptible dog is better than to be dead
and gone . . . however great people may have thought you
were. When life ceases, so ceases the opportunity to learn
wisdom. A dead man's portion is already done (vv. 4–6).
When life is over, so is the opportunity for repentance.

### I will meditate in thy statutes.

⁷Go thy way, eat thy bread with joy, and drink thy wine
with a merry heart; for God now accepteth thy works.
⁸Let thy garments be always white; and let thy head lack
no ointment. ⁹Live joyfully with the wife whom thou
lovest all the days of the life of thy vanity, which he hath
given thee under the sun, all the days of thy vanity: for
that is thy portion in this life, and in thy labour which
thou takest under the sun. (Eccl. 9:7–9)

The conclusion, again, can only come from the hand

of the sovereign God. He is the only one who can give
such a glorious gift in this futile world. "Go your
way . . ." The reason for the admonition is clear. "God
has *already* accepted your works" (v. 7). We begin with
justification, and then proceed to how we are to grow in
our sanctification—according to His Word.

The content of what we are to do in this sanctification is clear. First, we are to eat our bread (v. 7), and we
are to do it with joy. Secondly, we are to drink our wine
with a merry heart. The word for wine, incidentally, is
*yayin*—alcoholic drink. Our dress should be constantly
festive. We should take care of ourselves.

Turning to relationships, Solomon says that men
are to live *joyfully* with their wives for all their stupid
little days. We think this would sound terrible on an
anniversary card—because we are governed more by
sentiment than by wisdom. How is this possible? Apart
from the grace of God it is *not* possible.

The language of sentimental romanticism is not the
language of the Bible. When men understand the futility
of earthly existence, and they understand it in the way
Solomon presents it to us, they are then equipped to
enjoy their bread for perhaps the first time. They may
consider the redness of the wine and laugh over it with a
wise and contented joy. They may turn to love their
wives, not because sexual love is forever, but rather
because it is *not*. In the world of creatures, we may only
enjoy what we do not worship.

But we cannot rejoice in our silly lives until we
understand that it is our portion assigned to us by an
infinite wisdom. We cannot really understand that it is
our portion until we have faith in the God who *apportions*.
These things which we are to enjoy are passed to us from

His hand. So here is the word of the Lord. God has approved your obedience already. With gratitude—eat your bread, drink your wine, dress in white, and make a little love to your wife.

### Overview and Review

First division (1:2–2:26): Satisfaction does not come from man.

Second division (3:1–5:20): God is sovereign over everything.

Third division (6:1–8:15): Because God is sovereign, He can give the power to enjoy vanity. Solomon applies this doctrine.

Fourth division (8:16–12:14): Various obstacles and discouragements are addressed. First subdivision (8:16–9:9): Remaining incongruities must not diminish our joy.

# Use Your Head, Friend

*For we know that the whole creation groaneth and travaileth in pain together until now.*

Romans 8:22

Given what we have been taught in this book of wisdom about life under the sun, and despite any remaining glitches or incongruities, we are to work very hard and do so with a grounded and honest good sense.

**Remember the word unto thy servant.**
[10]Whatsoever thy hand findeth to do, do it with thy might; for there is no work, nor device, nor knowledge, nor wisdom, in the grave, whither thou goest. [11]I returned, and saw under the sun, that the race is not to the swift, nor the battle to the strong, neither yet bread to the wise, nor yet riches to men of understanding, nor yet favour to men of skill; but time and chance happeneth to them all. [12]For man also knoweth not his time: as the fishes that are taken in an evil net, and as the birds that are caught in the snare; so are the sons of men snared in an evil time, when it falleth suddenly upon them. (Eccl. 9:10–12)

Time and chance each take their shot. We are to work hard *now*, because the night is coming when no man can work (9:10). We are called to the duty of work and not to the duty of predicting results. The Hebrew word for *chance* here (*pega*) does not refer to philosophical randomness, but simply means "occurrence." The event is not planned by *us*. As far as we are concerned, anything can happen.

To say that things happen by "chance," if we are using anything other than a figure of speech, is to be theologically and philosophically incoherent. Everything that happens is caused by something; the Bible teaches that it is caused by Someone. To say that something happens by chance is simply to confess our ignorance of the cause.

We want to have a measure of control; we want to be setting the odds ourselves. But Solomon knows that the results are not predictable by any of those who live under the sun. "Who would have thought . . . ?" The results of all our endeavors are completely in the hands of God.

The time when we must cease our labors will fall upon us (9:12). Death comes suddenly, so labor as though that night is coming . . . because it is.

### Thy word hath quickened me.

[13]This wisdom have I seen also under the sun, and it seemed great unto me: [14]There was a little city, and few men within it; and there came a great king against it, and besieged it, and built great bulwarks against it: [15]Now there was found in it a poor wise man, and he by his wisdom delivered the city; yet no man remembered that same poor man. [16]Then said I, Wisdom is better than strength: nevertheless the poor man's wisdom is de-

spised, and his words are not heard. [17]The words of wise men are heard in quiet more than the cry of him that ruleth among fools. [18]Wisdom is better than weapons of war: but one sinner destroyeth much good.
(Eccl. 9:13–18)

The lesson of this little narrated scenario can either be that of ingratitude or of advice not taken. The latter option should be preferred here. The wisdom of the man *could* have saved the city, but his advice was not taken. But wisdom is still better than folly, even when it remains in the sheath. The voice of the wise is better than a shouting demagogue—but one sinner can still make a big mess.

### Yet have I not declined from thy law.
[1]Dead flies cause the ointment of the apothecary to send forth a stinking savour: so doth a little folly him that is in reputation for wisdom and honour. (Eccl. 10:1)

We now come to an onslaught of proverbs. Solomon hammers his point home again and again with many nails, as he mentions later (12:11). Work hard, he says, before the Lord, and with an honest *good sense*. The proverbs spur us on to this good sense.

Dead flies in the ointment have a lesson to teach (10:1). A little folly in a wise man is far more visible than a little wisdom in a fool. A wise man clearly has more to lose. Catsup on a white shirt is highly visible.

### I remembered thy judgments of old.
[2]A wise man's heart is at his right hand; but a fool's heart at his left. [3]Yea also, when he that is a fool walketh by

the way, his wisdom faileth him, and he saith to every
one that he is a fool. (Eccl. 10:2–3)

Wisdom comes out at the fingertips (10:2). Wisdom exhibits a careful dexterity, while folly fumbles.
Folly maintains a high profile (10:3). A fool can't walk
down the street without bumbling. As we live and
breathe, we broadcast what we are. If we are foolish, the
folks see us coming. If we are wise, that competence is
visible as well.

### Thy statutes have been my songs.

[4]If the spirit of the ruler rise up against thee, leave not
thy place; for yielding pacifieth great offences. [5]There is
an evil which I have seen under the sun, as an error which
proceedeth from the ruler: [6]Folly is set in great dignity,
and the rich sit in low place. [7]I have seen servants upon
horses, and princes walking as servants upon the earth.
(Eccl. 10:4–7)

Keeping your head is important (10:4). A wise
courtier does not panic at the first sign of trouble. This
is good, because stupidity generally has the run of high
places (10:5–7). Egalitarianism proceeds *from the top*, and
a denial of nobility is the folly of nobles. Such an
egalitarian spirit has been dominant in the West since
the time of the French Revolution, and to question the
rightness of it may cause this small book to come under
some official ban or other.

But though all men stand before the judgment seat
of Christ on the same footing, and although our courts
of justice should reflect that same impartiality, the fact
remains that some men and women are superior to other

men and women. Some are noble, and some are not. Some
are intelligent, and some are not. While all bear the image
of God, it is not the case that everyone has the same gifts
or abilities. It is a peculiar folly of some nobles to deny
the obvious and to seek to enthrone the common man all
in the name of "the people." In its modern manifestation,
we call it democracy. In its ancient garb, Solomon called
it foolishness.

Our egalitarianism requires herculean efforts from
us as we try to reconcile our dogma with the way the
world was established. This folly of egalitarianism is the
fountainhead of most of our modern *isms*—feminism,
socialism, fascism, racism, communism, *etc.* As the poet
said, beware all isms except for prisms.

### I have remembered thy name, O Lord.

[8]He that diggeth a pit shall fall into it; and whoso
breaketh an hedge, a serpent shall bite him. [9]Whoso
removeth stones shall be hurt therewith; and he that
cleaveth wood shall be endangered thereby. [10]If the iron
be blunt, and he do not whet the edge, then must he put
to more strength: but wisdom is profitable to direct.
(Eccl. 10:8–10)

The world is full of recoil action (10:8–9). We
must conduct our work with heads up. Danger lurks
everywhere. It is good to work smartly (10:10). We see
in this proverb a little Solomonic understatement. That
boy is trying to chop down a tree with a baseball bat.

If a man stopped to sharpen the ax, he would get
through the cord of wood a little faster. If he undertook
a little maintainance, the car would run longer. If he

thought ahead, he would not be surprised by inscrutable disasters and problems as often.

**I have said that I would keep thy words.**
[11]Surely the serpent will bite without enchantment; and a babbler is no better. (Eccl. 10:11)

It is good to be wary. A babbler should always be handled like a dangerous snake. A babbler *is* a dangerous snake. The tongue is a restless fire, ignited by hell. The problem need not be driven by malice; a verbal scribbler can do a lot of damage as well. Many lives are torn apart with the tongue.

**I turned my feet unto thy testimonies.**
[12]The words of a wise man's mouth are gracious; but the lips of a fool will swallow up himself. [13]The beginning of the words of his mouth is foolishness: and the end of his talk is mischievous madness. [14]A fool also is full of words: a man cannot tell what shall be; and what shall be after him, who can tell him? (Eccl. 10:12–14)

Empty chatter goes nowhere. A fool begins with lunacy and ends with imbecility—and has quite a trip in between. The words of the wise are in sharp contrast to this.

Fools are garrulous. The plain facts may be set before him, but he does not take them in. We cannot tell the future, but who can communicate that to a fool? He persists in buying books that solemnly foretell the future, usually from evangelical bookstores that specialize in eschatology, marks of the beast, computers

in Belgium, and those little bar code thingies that
Safeway uses.

*I have not forgotten thy law.*
¹⁵The labour of the foolish wearieth every one of them,
because he knoweth not how to go to the city.
(Eccl. 10:15)

Some are overwhelmed by nothing. We see here
some more understatement. That boy could get lost on
an escalator.

*I am a companion of all them that fear thee.*
¹⁶Woe to thee, O land, when thy king is a child, and thy
princes eat in the morning! ¹⁷Blessed art thou, O land,
when thy king is the son of nobles, and thy princes eat in
due season, for strength, and not for drunkenness!
(Eccl. 10:16–17)

A wasted nobility comes from a *wasted* nobility.
Beware of princes and presidents who like fast women
and cocaine.

*Teach me thy statutes.*
¹⁸By much slothfulness the building decayeth; and
through idleness of the hands the house droppeth
through. (Eccl. 10:18)

A lazy boy comes to nothing. Laziness destroys, but
the fool can't see it. His eyes are shut, as it turns out.

**Teach me good judgment and knowledge.**
[19]A feast is made for laughter, and wine maketh merry:
but money answereth all things. (Eccl. 10:19)

Money, as the fellow said, talks. Feasting and wine
have their limitations under the sun. Money doesn't. In
this Solomon is resorting to *overstatement.*

**I have believed thy commandments.**
[20]Curse not the king, no not in thy thought; and curse
not the rich in thy bedchamber: for a bird of the air shall
carry the voice, and that which hath wings shall tell the
matter. (Eccl. 10:20)

Then, as now, the walls had ears. Prudence requires
that we guard our tongues concerning those in power. A
little bird might talk to the *Washington Post,* and I am very
sorry about the comments I made earlier about presidents, fast women, and cocaine. Just a little homiletical
illustration.

**Their heart is as fat as grease; but I delight in
thy law.**
[1]Cast thy bread upon the waters: for thou shalt find it
after many days. [2]Give a portion to seven, and also to
eight; for thou knowest not what evil shall be upon the
earth. (Eccl. 11:1–2)

The business of generosity is governed by the Lord
with predictable results. Casting your bread on the water
is not about feeding the ducks. Solomon urges us to
treat alms like a business, investing in the Lord. The one
who gives to the poor is in fact giving to the Lord.

Thinking backwards can be fun sometimes (11:2). Some say that life is uncertain, so we should eat dessert first. Solomon says here that because life is uncertain we ought to give the dessert away.

### Give me understanding that I may learn.

[3]If the clouds be full of rain, they empty themselves upon the earth: and if the tree fall toward the south, or toward the north, in the place where the tree falleth, there it shall be. (Eccl. 11:3)

There it is, he says. Take life as it comes. There it is. And here you are. I had a delightful picture of the meaning of Ecclesiastes just a few months ago. I was looking at the road which runs by the front of our property, and a fellow in a pick-up truck was headed industriously south. "Well," I thought. "There he goes!"

### I have hoped in thy word.

[4]He that observeth the wind shall not sow; and he that regardeth the clouds shall not reap. (Eccl. 11:4)

When it comes to work, just hit it. Excuses are always plentiful. Too hot. Too cold. Too late.

### Thy judgments are right.

[5]As thou knowest not what is the way of the spirit, nor how the bones do grow in the womb of her that is with child: even so thou knowest not the works of God who maketh all. [6]In the morning sow thy seed, and in the evening withhold not thine hand: for thou knowest not whether shall prosper, either this or that, or whether they both shall be alike good. (Eccl. 11:5–6)

*Use Your Dead Friend*

Remember your limitations (11:5–6). God controls and makes everything, and He has not made us privy to the details. Recognize what you do not know (which is pretty much everything), and turn to what you *do* know (your assigned duties). Work hard at those duties because you don't know what will happen, whether you turn right or left.

And always remember that Ecclesiastes is at war with the folly of self-sufficiency. The key to wisdom is coming to understand what we do not know.

### Overview and Review

First division (1:2–2:26): Satisfaction is not *ex nihilo*.

Second division (3:1–5:20): Sovereignty is the Lord's. Solomon answers the objections to *that* idea.

Third division (6:1–8:15): Enjoyment of vanity is the gift of God.

Fourth division (8:16–12:14): The last section deals with various problems. First subdivision (8:16–9:9): Certainly, remaining incongruities must not diminish our joy in any way. Second subdivision (9:10–11:6): We must work hard and be sensible despite the situation.

# Geezer Time

*The righteous shall flourish like the palm tree: he shall grow like a*
*cedar in Lebanon. Those that be planted in the house of the LORD*
*shall flourish in the courts of our God. They shall still bring forth*
*fruit in old age; they shall be fat and flourishing; to shew that the*
*LORD is upright: he is my rock, and there is no unrighteousness in*
*him.*

Psalm 92:12–15

Solomon now brings us to a very important intro-
duction to the subject of old age. A wise preparation for
this begins long before, in the days of our youth.

### Thy law is my delight.

[7]Truly the light is sweet, and a pleasant thing it is for the
eyes to behold the sun: [8]But if a man live many years, and
rejoice in them all; yet let him remember the days of
darkness; for they shall be many. All that cometh is
vanity. [9]Rejoice, O young man, in thy youth; and let thy
heart cheer thee in the days of thy youth, and walk in the
ways of thine heart, and in the sight of thine eyes: but
know thou, that for all these things God will bring thee
into judgment. [10]Therefore remove sorrow from thy

heart, and put away evil from thy flesh: for childhood and youth are vanity. [1]Remember now thy Creator in the days of thy youth, while the evil days come not, nor the years draw nigh, when thou shalt say, I have no pleasure in them; [2]While the sun, or the light, or the moon, or the stars, be not darkened, nor the clouds return after the rain. (Eccl. 11:7–12:2)

The injunction is clear—enjoy and obey. Solomon turns to the young and encourages them to do two things—one characteristic of their age, and the other not. First he says, "Enjoy it now." The light of day and the vigor of youth are truly sweet. *Enjoy it* (v. 7). For the young, this advice is easy to follow.

And then he hits a more somber note—"while you can." A man who rejoices for many *years* must still prepare for the coming many *days* . . . days of darkness and vanity (v. 8). We cannot get away from age by lying to ourselves about it; we must receive it from the hand of God—and with a clear head.

He comes to "the conclusion." In a number of ways, the young are told both to *embrace* youth and *reject* evil. The young are called to be full of beans and *righteous*. Rejoice in your youth, he says, and remember the judgment of God (v. 9). Remove sorrow, and remove evil (v. 10). Although our youth is vanity, it must be enjoyed. This enjoyment is only possible if you remember your Creator *now*, before the difficult days arrive (12:1–2).

**I will meditate in thy precepts.**
[3]In the day when the keepers of the house shall tremble, and the strong men shall bow themselves, and the

grinders cease because they are few, and those that look
out of the windows be darkened, ⁴And the doors shall be
shut in the streets, when the sound of the grinding is
low, and he shall rise up at the voice of the bird, and all
the daughters of musick shall be brought low; ⁵Also
when they shall be afraid of that which is high, and fears
shall be in the way, and the almond tree shall flourish,
and the grasshopper shall be a burden, and desire shall
fail: because man goeth to his long home, and the
mourners go about the streets: ⁶Or ever the silver cord
be loosed, or the golden bowl be broken, or the pitcher
be broken at the fountain, or the wheel broken at the
cistern. ⁷Then shall the dust return to the earth as it was:
and the spirit shall return unto God who gave it.
(Eccl. 12:3–7)

So we come to the fall of a great house. Solomon
brings us to an extended analogy, depicting the problems
associated with the onslaught of old age. He compares
the body falling apart to the distress of a great house in
increasing disrepair.

The "housekeepers" fail (12:3). Hands and arms
tremble because of feebleness or palsy. The "strong men"
struggle (12:3). The legs bend under the weight of age.
The "grinders" no longer perform their appointed work
(12:3). The teeth lose their ability to chew.

It starts getting too dark, too dark to see (12:3).
The eyes lose their sight. The doors are "closed" (12:4).
The mouth folds in due to lack of teeth. All you can hear
are "soft sounds" (12:4). The sound of chewing is low.

Another problem comes, that of "sleeping lightly"
(12:4). The elderly are notorious for sleeping lightly.

The "daughters of music" depart (12:4). Ability to enjoy music declines.

A new fear enters, a "fear of heights" (12:5). Those who are old now fear stumbling and falling. A fall would have far worse consequences than it ever had before.

The "almond tree" blossoms (12:5). The hair is now white or gray. The person afflicted is a "lame grasshopper" (12:5). The legs now bend under the weight of age.

Of course we see sexual decline (12:5). Desire for sexual activity and satisfaction fails. The Hebrew here is "the caperberry [an aphrodesiac] fails." All the old tricks don't work anymore. This is particularly difficult news for our modern prophets and apostles of sexual autonomy. But it does not really matter if they like it or not; a time is coming when this particular idol is all done.

All such things are preparation for dying and death (12:5). Before that time arrives, *remember your Creator* (v. 6). And so death comes (12:6). The obscure images here all clearly indicate the point of the marvelous creation of the human body . . . breaking. The dust of our bodies will return to its source, and our spirits will go to God (v. 7).

**Let my heart be sound in thy statutes.**
[8]Vanity of vanities, saith the preacher; all is vanity. [9]And moreover, because the preacher was wise, he still taught the people knowledge; yea, he gave good heed, and sought out, and set in order many proverbs. [10]The preacher sought to find out acceptable words: and that which was written was upright, even words of truth. [11]The words of the wise are as goads, and as nails fas-

tened by the masters of assemblies, which are given from one shepherd. ¹²And further, by these, my son, be admonished: of making many books there is no end; and much study is a weariness of the flesh. (Eccl. 12:8–12)

This release from vanity is . . . vanity (v. 8). The teaching we receive in Ecclesiastes is not random—the proverbs were set in order, and they taught the people knowledge (v. 9). This book is most emphatically *not* one of nihilistic despair—these are words of truth (v. 10). Solomon tells us that we have been provoked by him into wisdom, and that these nails have been placed with precision, and all directed by God (v. 11). Those who would repent of their folly must let Solomon nail it down for them.

And, he reminds us, if we have not been mastered by a short book like this one, the long line of remaining big fat books will be nothing but weariness in the head (v. 12).

### Overview and Review

First division (1:2–2:26): Satisfaction is not in us.

Second division (3:1–5:20): God is sovereign over everything. Objections answered.

Third division (6:1–8:15): Solomon applies the doctrine that God gives enjoyment in vanity.

Fourth division (8:16–12:14): Various obstacles and discouragements are addressed. First subdivision (8:16–9:9): Remaining incongruities must not diminish our joy. Second subdivision (9:10–11:6): We must work hard and sensibly despite remaining incongruities. Third subdivision (11:7–12:12): We must prepare for our long journey through old age and into eternity.

# Conclusion

*And there are also many other things which Jesus did, the which, if they should be written every one, I suppose that even the world itself could not contain the books that should be written. Amen.*

John 21:25

**So shall I keep the testimony of thy mouth.**
[13]Let us hear the conclusion of the whole matter: Fear God, and keep his commandments: for this is the whole duty of man. [14]For God shall bring every work into judgment, with every secret thing, whether it be good, or whether it be evil (Eccl. 12:13–14).

And so Solomon wraps it up. Here is the conclusion of the whole thing—this is where we have come at the end of the argument. Fear God, Solomon argues, and do what He says. This is our portion and our all, and when we receive it, we receive joy from His hand.

We must note that this is his *conclusion*. What he brings us to at this place follows from his premises. For those who have not followed the argument, it is tempting to say that Solomon has simply thrown up his hands in existential despair and taken a leap of edifying faith. But he has not. Remembrance of the final judgment is the conclusion of his argument, and we must remember that Solomon's powers of argument were considerable.

So God will judge the secret things, all of them, whether good or evil. But how can the thought of exhaustive judgment bring pleasure and encouragement anywhere, especially in the midst of vanity?

Here is the word of the Lord—*it is the gift of God.*

# Notes

## De Profundis
† No footnotes here. This chapter spoke for itself.

## The Meaning of Joy
[1] If the book of Ecclesiastes presented vanity to mean utter and ultimate absurdity, then it would have had much less argumentation in it and more references to buttered toast, rainbow trout, along with veiled prophecies of attempts at poetry by Walt Whitman. This would be far more consistent with the "absurdity worldview," which would, of course, make it inconsistent.

[2] I am greatly indebted to Walter Kaiser for this procedure and for his treatment of the translation issues in Eccl. 2:24–26. See his small but very fine commentary on Ecclesiastes. Walter Kaiser, *Ecclesiastes: Total Life* (Chicago, IL: Moody Press, 1979), p. 43–45.

## A Taste of Nothing
[1] A good representation of this kind of thinking can be found in Clark Pinnock's work and other "openness of God" types. Completely apart from the heresy

involved in this tiny god approach, when the argument of
Ecclesiastes as a whole is considered, another fundamen-
tal problem should come to mind. This heresy is not just
wrong-headed, it is wrong-hearted. It is a doctrinal
killjoy. The fact that this is a stuffed shirt theology
needs no further documentation than the fact that
InterVarsity Press is now publishing this stuff.

² The issue in all this is brain fog, which is why the
discussion has nothing at all to do with caffeine, tobacco,
or ice cream. Nevertheless, because tobacco is now on the
fast track to being declared a drug by our federal masters, it is important for us to think biblically here as
well. The drugs addressed earlier are all mind-altering
drugs. With coffee and tobacco, and anything else we
might think of, the issue is not the loss of reason,
because these are not mind-altering agents. But another
issue, one that is none of the magistrate's business
either, is the loss of joy. The body is hard enough to
subdue (Rom. 6:12) without giving it a bunch of extra
dependencies. I will not be brought, Paul says, under the
power of *any* (1 Cor. 6:12–13). But if his joy is not held
hostage by whatever it may be, he may follow the example of many of God's most effective servants, thank
God for that fine creature tobacco, and smoke like a
chimney to the glory of God.

### The End of the Tether

† Of course, in this vain world, *he couldn't care less*
means the same thing as *he could care less.* And *don't be
surprised if he doesn't get better* means that we shouldn't be
surprised if he does.

## Beautiful in Its Time

† No footnotes here either. Sorry.

## The Silence of Despair

† A number of years ago a friend of mine made an off-hand comment which might appear to some to reflect a deficient faith in American democracy. He said, "Of course he's corrupt. He's running for president, isn't he?" Time has passed, and I would want to modify his comment only slightly. A number of people, Christians particularly, when they first enter our political process, are in fact not yet corrupt. They have seen the problems with our public life and they want to make a difference. Our botched public affairs finally get enough sideways that some unsullied souls spit on their hands and determine to get in there and make this thing work. This, as H. L. Mencken once observed, is like thinking that "the remedy for prostitution is to fill the bawdy houses with virgins."

Still, it can't be helped. The sun goes up and the sun goes down, and a society in decline will never have a shortage of reformers and patriots clustering round. They either fail and keep their purity, or they succeed and discover that this whole thing is more complex than previously thought. After all, they came in to make a difference, and they can't make a difference unless they stay around, and they can't stay around unless they learn to play the game. Miss Realistic is quite a seductive little thing, but she always has ugly babies. When the cancer of corruption is well-advanced in a commonwealth, believers can easily be maneuvered into festooning themselves with the campaign buttons of the less corrupt. Such relative comparisons between "horrible" and "not quite so bad" can appear quite stark, and they do give political campaigns a high entertainment value, but they still do not reflect the standards of the law of God.

### A Sacrifice of Fools
† When you don't have anything to say, don't say it.

### Tiny Little Souls and Tight Little Shoes
† The writer was Malcolm Muggeridge, but I can't remember where he said it.

### Walking in the Corridors of Power
¹ Francis Bellamy, a socialist minister, first published the Pledge of Allegiance in 1892. School children first recited it at the dedication of the 1892 Chicago World's Fair. In 1945, the Pledge was adopted by the 79th Congress, and in 1954 the words *under God* were added to the Pledge. And the object of the Pledge, the flag of these United States, may now be offered protection by means of an amendment to the Constitution prohibiting flag burning. The proposed amendment, like the Pledge, represents a well-intentioned misunderstanding of the meaning of true loyalty.

Consider the word *indivisible*. The word does not reflect a charitable desire—"may the nation never be divided." Rather, the word means "incapable of being divided." This represents an ontological claim and goes far beyond a scriptural desire for political stability. The same distinction can be observed between the vain pagan dream, "May the king live forever," and the Christian desire and hope, "Long live the king."

The problem with the claim is that it is just not true. Our nation, like every nation among men, is capable of

division. We may oppose or support such division if and
when it happens, but all should agree that it is most
certainly not an impossibility. But if it is not an impossibility, then why do we claim that it is? The Confederates
and the Yankees had different views on the desirability of
separation, but they did agree on one thing. They agreed
that the thing could happen—that is why there was a
war. Anyone believing this nation is indivisible will treat
all attempts at secession as the civic equivalent of a
perpetual motion machine.

Our culture is currently in rebellion against the laws
of Heaven. The Bible tells us that a throne is established
by righteousness; a throne is not established by making
schoolchildren say untrue things, or by putting people in
the chokey if they burn the flag. Thrones are not established by pledges or penalties. Scripture tells us that a
nation is blessed whose God is the Lord. The Bible says,
"Take away the dross from the silver, and there shall
come forth a vessel for the finer. Take away the wicked
from before the king, and his throne shall be established
in righteousness" (Prov. 25:4–5). Christians must be
loyal citizens. But they must first understand the ground
of all allegiance.

[2] Some try to tell us that capital punishment does
not have a deterrent value. But certainly, at a minimum,
does it not deter the one executed?

## Loving Your Wife

[†] I know, most of this chapter wasn't about marriage.